QUICK

BIBLE
GUIDE

A SIMPLE INTRO TO EVERY BOOK IN SCRIPTURE

ERIC DYKSTRA

I dedicate this book to my Dad.
He would have been so proud to see me write
a book explaining each book of the Bible.
He was a lifelong learner.
I know he is cheering me on from Heaven.
Thanks Dad, for all you taught me.
I'll see you in Heaven soon. I miss you.

TABLE OF CONTENTS

INTRODUCTION
A CHEAT SHEET FOR THE BIBLE

Have you ever said to yourself, "I'm gonna try reading the Bible!" and then picked it up and realized *Holy Cow! This thing is enormous!*?

- How can anyone read a book this big?
- Where do I start - at the beginning like a normal book?
- Is the Bible more like a reference book and I just read what seems interesting to me?
- What do I *do* with this ginormous book?

If you have asked those questions, you are not alone. When I first became a Christ-follower, I had all those questions and so many more! I'll be honest - The Bible was a really big book to me at first. It was so intimidating. In the New King James Version, there are 770,430 words! There are 31,102 verses and 1,189 chapters in the Old and New Testament!

Who reads a book with 1,189 chapters?!

Pretty much no one except NERDS (and lawyers, but I think that is pretty much the same thing).

Anyway, lots of people WANT to read the Bible, but they get intimated by its size and wordiness. And so, they never get around to actually doing it. That is why I created the BIBLE: COVER TO COVER teaching series at our church that has now become the easy reference guide you're holding in your hands.

Once I went to Bible college and learned this important information, Scripture became less intimidating. I want to help the average person know this stuff, too! So I set out to create a cheat guide with all the necessary background information of each of the 66 books of Scripture, so the Bible would not seem so complicated and people could study it and apply its truth.

My goal was to make a big book feel accessible. So, for each book, I tried to explain the important information before you read it:

- Who the author is
- When the book was written
- What type of literature the book is
- The big idea or concept of the book
- A couple of key verses or themes
- How to apply it
- And any other important information the reader should know before studying that particular book

Also, in the Old Testament I pointed out where Jesus can be found in every book. In the New Testament I didn't need to do that because it was obvious.

So that's the basic idea of this guide. It is a simple cheat sheet on Scripture so reading it will be less intimidating and much more accessible.

Now give it shot!

Pick the Bible book you want to study. Before you study it, read the cheat sheet in this guide, then go read the Bible. I hope and pray it helps.

I dare you to read it! That big book will change your life! It did mine.

THE BIBLE 101:

Learning the Basics of the World's Greatest Book

PART 1: WHY STUDY THE BIBLE?

1. **When we study God's Word, our lives are better off.**

   Joshua 1:8 Keep this Book of the Law always on your lips; meditate on it day and night, so that you may be careful to do everything written in it. Then you will be prosperous and successful. (NIV)

2. **When we study God's Word, we become better people.**

   2 Timothy 3:16-17 All Scripture is inspired by God and is useful to teach us what is true and to make us realize what is wrong in our lives. It corrects us when we are wrong and teaches us to do what is right. God uses it to prepare and equip his people to do every good work. (NLT)

3. **When we study God's Word, we get better direction.**

   Psalms 119:105 Your word is a lamp to my feet and a light to my path.

4. **When we study God's Word, we develop a better relationship with Jesus.**

   John 20:31 ...these are written so that you may continue to believe that Jesus is the Messiah, the Son of God, and that by believing in him you will have life by the power of his name. (NLT)

   Revelation 19:13 His name [Jesus] is the Word of God. (NIV)

PART 2: WHAT'S IN THE BIBLE?

The Bible is a library, not a regular book.

There are 39 books in the Old Testament
and 27 books in the New Testament.

It is composed of stories, songs, sermons, and epistles (or letters).

In the Old Testament, you can read books about the Israelites and also songs/poems. There are also sermons from major prophets (larger books) and minor prophets (smaller books).

In the New Testament, the gospels are stories about Jesus. Acts tells the history of the first church, and the Book of Revelation is prophecy about the future.

Here is a handy chart for reference:

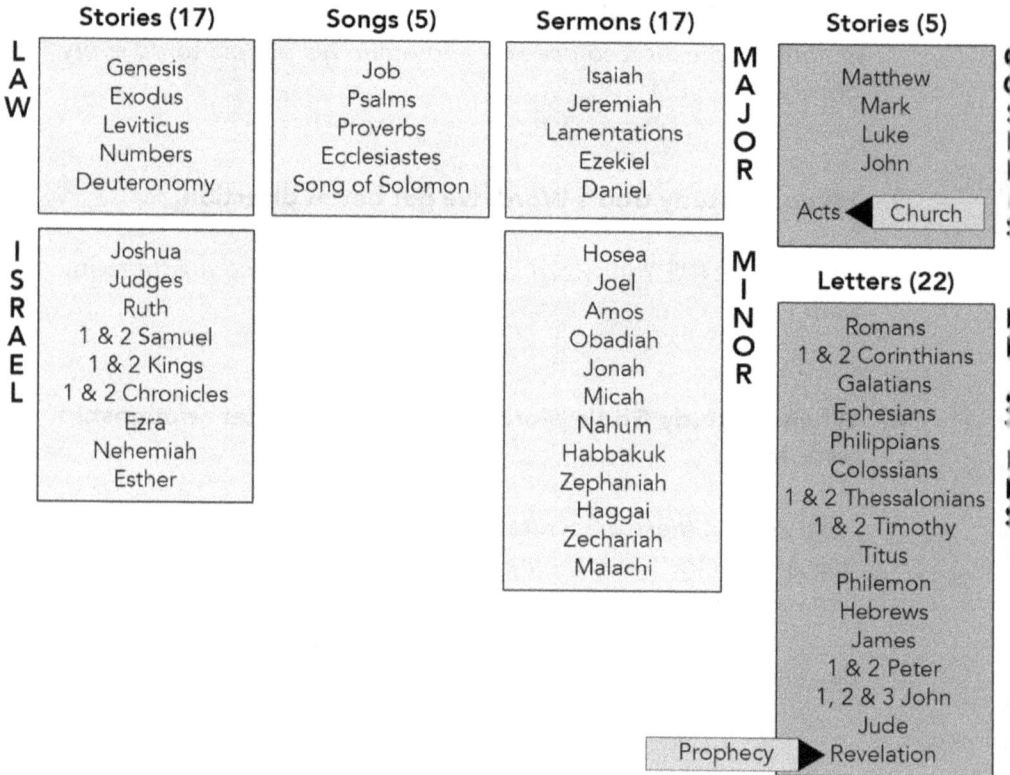

Stories (17)	Songs (5)	Sermons (17)		Stories (5)
Genesis Exodus Leviticus Numbers Deuteronomy	Job Psalms Proverbs Ecclesiastes Song of Solomon	Isaiah Jeremiah Lamentations Ezekiel Daniel	M A J O R	Matthew Mark Luke John

L A W / I S R A E L

Acts ◄ Church

		Hosea Joel Amos Obadiah Jonah Micah Nahum Habbakuk Zephaniah Haggai Zechariah Malachi	M I N O R	

Joshua
Judges
Ruth
1 & 2 Samuel
1 & 2 Kings
1 & 2 Chronicles
Ezra
Nehemiah
Esther

Letters (22)

Romans
1 & 2 Corinthians
Galatians
Ephesians
Philippians
Colossians
1 & 2 Thessalonians
1 & 2 Timothy
Titus
Philemon
Hebrews
James
1 & 2 Peter
1, 2 & 3 John
Jude

Prophecy ► Revelation

PART 3: HOW DO I STUDY THE BIBLE FOR MYSELF?

PREP: A simple way to study your Bible every day.

- **P**ray - Ask the Holy Spirit to speak to you!

- **R**ead - Read the suggested verses for that day.

- **E**xplore - Ask yourself 3 questions:

  1. What does this tell me about God?

  2. What does this tell me about people?

  3. How can I apply this to my life today?

- **P**ractice - Go and do what the Bible said to do.

A note: you can't understand the Bible if the Holy Spirit is not in you.

> *2 Corinthians 4:4 Satan, who is the god of this world, has blinded the minds of those who don't believe. They are unable to see the glorious light of the Good News. They don't understand this message about the glory of Christ... (NLT)*
>
> *I Corinthians 2:14 ...people who aren't spiritual can't receive these truths from God's Spirit. It all sounds foolish to them and they can't understand it, for only those who are spiritual can understand what the Spirit means.*

You can pray a simple prayer to receive Jesus and allow the Holy Spirit to illuminate the Scriptures so you can understand them. Pray something like this:

Jesus, I believe You died and rose again to forgive me for all my sins. I give You the leadership of my life. I ask the Holy Spirit to move inside me to help me understand Your Word. In Jesus' name, Amen.

GENESIS

Book: 1 of 66

Author: Moses

Type of Literature: History. Genesis is the origin story of our universe, mankind, and our faith.

Date of Writing: 1446-1406 B.C. Moses wrote Genesis during the 40 years of wilderness wandering after Israel left Egypt following the 10 plagues.

Time Period Covered: Creation – 1446 BC. The word Genesis in Hebrew is "Beginnings".

Key verse: *Genesis 1:1 In the beginning God...*

BIG IDEA OF GENESIS:
Genesis is the foundation of our faith and worldview.

1. Foundation of the universe. *Genesis 1:1*

2. Foundation of mankind. *Genesis 1:26*

3. Foundation for sexual identity. *Genesis 1:27*

4. Foundation of marriage. *Genesis 2:21-22, 24*

5. Foundation of sin & brokenness. *Genesis 3:6-7; Romans 3:23; Romans 8:22*

6. Foundation of salvation. *Genesis 3:15*

7. Foundation of geology. *Genesis 7:11; Genesis 7:19-20*

8. Foundation of the races. *Genesis 9:18-19; Genesis 11:9*

9. Foundation of the faithful.

    - Abraham - *Genesis 12-25*
    - Isaac - *Genesis 21-28, 35*
    - Jacob - *Genesis 25-37, 42-43, 45-49*
    - Joseph - *Genesis 37-50*

✝ JESUS IN GENESIS

1. Jesus is the God who creates us.

Genesis 1:1-3 In the beginning God created the heavens and the earth.

Colossians 1:16 For by Him (Jesus) all things were created that are in heaven and that are on earth, visible and invisible, whether thrones or dominions or principalities or powers. All things were created through Him and for Him.

2. Jesus is the God who walks with us.

Genesis 3:8 When the cool evening breezes were blowing, the man and his wife heard the LORD God walking about in the garden. (NLT)

Genesis 5:22 Enoch walked with God three hundred years.

John 1:18 No one has ever seen God, but the one and only Son, who is himself God and is in closest relationship with the Father, has made him known. (NIV)

3. Jesus is the God who offers salvation to us.

Genesis 7:15-16 Two by two they came into the boat, representing every living thing that breathes... Then the Lord closed the door behind them. (NLT)

John 10:9 I am the door. If anyone enters by Me, he will be saved, and will go in and out and find pasture.

4. Jesus is the God who sacrificed Himself for us.

Genesis 22:2 Then He said, "Take now your son, your only son Isaac, whom you love, and go to the land of Moriah, and offer him there as a burnt offering on one of the mountains of which I shall tell you."

John 3:16 ...this is how God loved the world: He gave his one and only Son, so that everyone who believes in him will not perish but have eternal life. (NLT)

5. Jesus is the God who will rule victorious for us.

Genesis 49:9-10 Judah, my son, is a young lion that has finished eating its prey. Like a lion he crouches and lies down; like a lioness— who dares to rouse him? The scepter will not depart from Judah, nor the ruler's staff from his descendants, until the coming of the one to whom it belongs, the one whom all nations will honor. (NLT)

Revelation 5:5-6a But one of the elders said to me, "Do not weep. Behold, the Lion of the tribe of Judah, the Root of David, has prevailed... And I looked, and behold, in the midst of the throne and of the four living creatures, and in the midst of the elders, stood a Lamb as though it had been slain.

LET'S APPLY IT!

You get to choose what you believe about origins. You can believe you are an accident of nature in a purposeless universe, or you can believe that a loving God made you, died for you, wants to be with you, and has a good plan for you.

What will you believe?

EXODUS

Book: 2 of 66

Author: Moses

Type of Literature: History. Exodus is the story of Israel's exit from slavery.

Date of Writing: 1446-1406 B.C. Moses wrote Exodus sometime after Israel left Egypt following the 10 plagues.

Time Period Covered: 1446-1440 B.C. From the 10 plagues to the 10 commandments.

Key verse: *Exodus 6:7 I will claim you as my own people, and I will be your God. Then you will know that I am the Lord your God who has freed you from your oppression in Egypt. (NLT)*

BIG IDEA OF EXODUS:
God saves His people from slavery.

Exodus 14:13-14 And Moses said to the people, "Do not be afraid. Stand still, and see the salvation of the Lord, which He will accomplish for you today. For the Egyptians whom you see today, you shall see again no more forever. The Lord will fight for you, and you shall hold your peace."

6 MAJOR MOMENTS IN EXODUS:

1. **BURNING BUSH - God sends Israel a deliverer.** *Exodus 3:2-6*

2. **YHWH - God explains His name for the first time. "I AM."** *Exodus 3:13-14*

3. **10 PLAGUES - God conquers Egypt & its false demon gods.** *Exodus 7-11; Deuteronomy 32:17; Ephesians 6:14*

4. **THE PASSOVER - God "passes over" those marked with the blood of a lamb.** *Exodus 12*

5. **PARTING THE RED SEA - God saves His people as they pass through the water.** *Exodus 14*

6. **10 Commandments - God gives His people spiritual guidelines for a good life.** *Exodus 20*

✝ JESUS IN EXODUS

1. Jesus is the God of the burning bush.

Exodus 3:13-14 But Moses protested, "If I go to the people of Israel and tell them, 'The God of your ancestors has sent me to you,' they will ask me, 'What is his name?' Then what should I tell them?" God replied to Moses, "I AM who I AM. Say this to the people of Israel: I AM has sent me to you."

John 8:58 Jesus said to them, "Most assuredly, I say to you, before Abraham was, I AM."

2. Jesus is our Passover Lamb.

Exodus 12:21, 23 Then Moses called all the elders of Israel together and said to them, "Go, pick out a lamb or young goat for each of your families, and slaughter the Passover animal.... For the LORD will pass through the land to strike down the Egyptians. But when he sees the blood on the top and sides of the doorframe, the LORD will pass over your home. He will not permit his death angel to enter your house and strike you down." (NLT)

1 Corinthians 5:7 ...Christ, our Passover Lamb, has been sacrificed for us. (NLT)

3. Jesus gives us grace instead of rules of stone.

John 1:16-17 And of His fullness we have all received, and grace for grace. For the law was given through Moses, but grace and truth came through Jesus Christ.

LET'S APPLY IT!

1. **We ALL need deliverance. (Like the Israelites were slaves in Egypt, we are all slaves to sin.)**

    John 8:34 Jesus replied, "I tell you the truth, everyone who sins is a slave of sin." (NLT)

2. **Jesus is our Deliverer. (Like Moses led Israel to freedom, Jesus leads us to freedom.)**

    John 8:36 ...if the Son sets you free, you will be free indeed. (NIV)

3. **We need the blood of Jesus over our lives. (Like Israel put the blood of a lamb on doorposts.)**

    I Peter 1:18-19 ...knowing that you were not redeemed with corruptible things, like silver or gold, from your aimless conduct received by tradition from your fathers, but with the precious blood of Christ, as of a lamb without blemish and without spot.

4. **We pass through the waters of baptism as a symbol of new life. (Like Israel passed through the water of the Red Sea to new life.)**

    Romans 6:4 Therefore we were buried with Him through baptism into death, that just as Christ was raised from the dead by the glory of the Father, even so we also should walk in newness of life.

5. **We rescue others caught in the slavery of sin. (Like Moses rescued Israel.)**

    We exist to help as many people as we can cross the line of faith and follow Jesus.

LEVITICUS

Book: 3 of 66

Author: Moses

Type of Literature: Law. This is ancient Israel's rule book of civic & moral laws in order to be in relationship with God.

Date of Writing: 1446-1406 B.C. Moses wrote Leviticus during the 40 years of wilderness wandering after Israel left Egypt.

Time Period Covered: 1446-1440 B.C.

Key verses:

Leviticus 19:2 You shall be holy, for I the LORD your God am holy.

Leviticus 20:26 Thus you are to be holy to Me, for I the LORD am holy; and I have set you apart from the peoples to be Mine. (NASB)

BIG IDEA OF LEVITICUS:
How sinful humans coexist with a holy God.

Simple outline of Leviticus:

- How to say "I'm sorry" with 5 different sacrifices (Leviticus 1-7)
- Priests are "set apart" as holy for ministry (Leviticus 8-10)
- How to live as holy people. Set apart - morals, families, devotional life & community (Leviticus 11-22)
- How to celebrate a holy feast, seven feasts to remember God's goodness (Leviticus 23-27)

MAJOR THEMES OF LEVITICUS

1. Holiness. Holy means set apart. To be a worshiper, we must see God as holy and pursue holiness ourselves.

Romans 12:1-2 And so, dear brothers and sisters, I plead with you to give your bodies to God because of all he has done for you. Let them be a living and holy sacrifice–the kind he will find acceptable.

This is truly the way to worship him. Don't copy the behavior and customs of this world, but let God transform you into a new person by changing the way you think. Then you will learn to know God's will for you, which is good and pleasing and perfect. (NLT)

2. **Sacrifice. To be forgiven of sin, blood must be spilled.**

Leviticus 17:11 ...the life of the flesh is in the blood, and I have given it to you upon the altar to make atonement for your souls; for it is the blood that makes atonement for the soul.

Hebrews 9:22 ...under the law almost everything is purified with blood, and without the shedding of blood there is no forgiveness of sins. (ESV)

3. **Offerings. To worship the Lord, offerings are voluntarily given.**

Leviticus 27:28 ...every <u>devoted</u> offering is most holy to the LORD.

2 Corinthians 9:7 Let each one give [thoughtfully and with purpose] just as he has decided in his heart, not grudgingly or under compulsion, for God loves a cheerful giver [and delights in the one whose heart is in his gift]. (AMP)

4. **Feasts. To live holy, happy lives, we schedule regular gratitude celebrations of God.**

A suggestion of celebrations for New Testament believers:
- Devote daily - Spend quality time in relationship with God in the Word and prayer.

- Withdraw weekly - Take one day each week to worship & rest.

- Abandon annually - Take one week each year to seek the Lord with your family.

- Celebrate seasonally - Christmas, Easter, Thanksgiving, etc. - make these gratitude days to the Lord, not just secular family days.

✝ JESUS IN LEVITICUS/LET'S APPLY IT!

1. **Jesus is our holy sacrifice, so we ask Him to cleanse us from sin.**

   I John 1:7,9 ...the blood of Jesus Christ His Son cleanses us from all sin. If we confess our sins, He is faithful and just <u>to forgive us</u> our sins and <u>to cleanse us</u> from all unrighteousness.

2. **Jesus is our holy High Priest, so we trust Him to help us overcome sin.**

   Hebrews 4:15 This High Priest of ours understands our weaknesses, for he faced all of the same testings we do, yet he did not sin. (NLT)

3. **Jesus is our holy focus, so we orbit our lives and families around worship, celebrations, gratitude, and praise.**

   Hebrews 3:1 Therefore, <u>holy brethren,</u> partakers of the heavenly calling, consider the Apostle and High Priest of our confession, Christ Jesus...

Book: 4 of 66

Author: Moses

Type of Literature: History. This book is a census (numbers) of Israel & their story of wandering in the wilderness for 40 years.

Date of Writing: 1440-1400 B.C. Moses wrote Numbers during the 40 years of wilderness wandering.

Time Period Covered: 1440-1400 B.C.

Key verse: *Numbers 14:8 If the LORD delights in us, then He will bring us into this land and give it to us, 'a land which flows with milk and honey.'*

BIG IDEA OF NUMBERS:
How to turn an 11-day walk into 40 years of wandering.

I Corinthians 10:6 These things happened as a warning to us, so that we would not crave evil things as they did. (NLT)

MAJOR THEMES OF NUMBERS:

1. **Complaining & rebellion.** *(Numbers 11:1, 11:4, 12:1, 14:1-2, 16:1-3, 16:41, 20:3, 21:5)*

   I Corinthians 10:10-11 ...don't grumble as some of them did, and then were destroyed by the angel of death. These things happened to them as examples for us. They were written down to warn us who live at the end of the age. (NLT)

   • Faith and complaining are both contagious.

2. **Lack of faith in God's promises and power.** *Numbers 14:1-4*

3. **Consequences for a lack of faith - an entire generation missed the Promised Land.** *Numbers 14:27b-35*

4. **God's mercy & grace.** *Numbers 14:18*

    2 Peter 3:9 The Lord is... patient toward you, not wishing that any should perish, but that all should reach repentance. (ESV)

5. **Caleb & Joshua's example of faith in God's promises & power.** *Numbers 14:6-9*

✝ JESUS IN NUMBERS

1. **The bronze serpent.**

    Numbers 21:6-9 [the people complained] ...So the Lord sent fiery serpents among the people, and they bit the people; and many of the people of Israel died. Therefore the people came to Moses, and said, "We have sinned, for we have spoken against the Lord and against you; pray to the Lord that He take away the serpents from us." So Moses prayed for the people. Then the Lord said to Moses, "Make a fiery serpent, and set it on a pole; and it shall be that everyone who is bitten, when he looks at it, shall live." So Moses made a bronze serpent, and put it on a pole; and so it was, if a serpent had bitten anyone, when he looked at the bronze serpent, he lived.

    John 3:14 ...as Moses lifted up the serpent in the wilderness, even so must the Son of Man be lifted up.

2. **Balaam's prophecy. (An evil man who was hired to curse Israel with witchcraft instead speaks a powerful prophecy of the coming of Jesus.)**

    Numbers 24:17 "I see Him, but not now; I behold Him, but not near; A Star shall come out of Jacob; A Scepter shall rise out of Israel, And batter the brow of Moab, And destroy all the sons of tumult."

LET'S APPLY IT!

1. **Speak faith. Don't complain or doubt God's promises or power. HE NEVER FAILS.**

    2 Corinthians 4:13 ...since we have the same spirit of faith, according to what is written, "I believed and therefore I spoke," we also believe and therefore speak.

2. **Show honor. Don't complain or rebel against your spiritual leaders. They are not perfect, but they are appointed by God to lead you.**

    I Thessalonians 5:12 Dear brothers and sisters, honor those who are your leaders in the Lord's work. They work hard among you and give you spiritual guidance. (NLT)

3. **Look at Jesus.**

    At any given moment, we are looking at 1 of 4 things:
    *   Circumstances - this will discourage you
    *   Others - this will make you jealous or cause rivalry and mistrust
    *   Self - this will cause pride or hopelessness
    *   Jesus - keep your eyes on Him. Only Jesus will get you through

    Hebrews 12:2 Let us fix our eyes on Jesus, the author and perfecter of our faith... (BSB)

DEUTERONOMY

Book: 5 of 66

Author: Moses

Type of Literature: Law. Deuteronomy means "second law". This is Moses' final sermon to the people of Israel. Much of it is a reminder of the law already given.

Date of Writing: 1408-1406 B.C. Moses wrote Deuteronomy at the end of his life when the 40 years of wilderness wandering was over.

Time Period Covered: 1408-1406 B.C.

Moses' Sermon Outline of Deuteronomy:

1. Remember how God led you out of Egypt (Deuteronomy 1-3). God is faithful.

2. Remember your relationship with God (Deuteronomy 4-10). God is relational.

3. Remember the law of God (Deuteronomy 11-26). God is holy.

4. Blessings & warnings (Deuteronomy 27-34). God gives you freedom of choice.

Key verses:

Deuteronomy 6:5 You shall love the LORD your God with all your heart, with all your soul, and with all your strength.

Deuteronomy 30:19-20 I call heaven and earth as witnesses today against you, that I have set before you life and death, blessing and cursing; therefore choose life, that both you and your descendants may live; that you may love the LORD your God, that you may obey His voice, and that you may cling to Him, for He is your life and the length of your days; and that you may dwell in the land which the Lord swore to your fathers, to Abraham, Isaac, and Jacob, to give them.

BIG IDEA OF DEUTERONOMY:
Every day is a choice. We can walk with God or away from God.

MAJOR THEMES IN DEUTERONOMY:

1. Love God: God desires relationship with you.

Deuteronomy 1:31 ...in the wilderness where you saw how the LORD your God carried you, as a man carries his son...

Deuteronomy 6:5 You shall love the LORD your God with all your heart, with all your soul, and with all your strength.

2. Teach your children: God wants your children to be in relationship with Him.

Deuteronomy 6:5-7 You shall love the LORD your God with all your heart, with all your soul, and with all your strength. And these words which I command you today shall be in your heart. You shall teach them diligently to your children, and shall talk of them when you sit in your house, when you walk by the way, when you lie down, and when you rise up.

- *Shall be in your heart* - Faith starts with mom & dad
- *Diligently* - Top priority
- *Sit in your house* - Not just go to worship, but your home is a house of worship
- *Walk by the way* - When you go to work and school or run errands
- *When you lie down* - Nightly prayer & Bible reading
- *When you rise up* - Morning prayer & Bible reading

3. Freedom of choice: You get to choose whether you want to walk with God or not.

Deuteronomy 30:19-20 I call heaven and earth as witnesses today against you, that I have set before you life and death, blessing and cursing; therefore choose life, that both you and your descendants may live; that you may love the LORD your God, that you may obey His voice, and that you may cling to Him, for He is your life and the length of your days; and that you may dwell in the land which the LORD swore to your fathers, to Abraham, Isaac, and Jacob, to give them."

✝ JESUS IN DEUTERONOMY

1. **Jesus' favorite book? Jesus quotes more from Deuteronomy than any other book.**

   For example: Jesus answers all 3 of His temptations from the devil with quotes from Deuteronomy (Luke 4:1–13).

2. **Moses' prophecy:**

   Deuteronomy 18:15 The LORD your God will raise up for you a prophet like me from among your fellow Israelites. You must listen to him. (NLT)

LET'S APPLY IT!

We must remember every day is a choice . Walking with God is not a one-time decision, but a daily decision.

What do you need to put into practice TODAY in order to walk with Jesus?

- Choose Jesus as Forgiver and Leader. *Romans 10:9-10*

- Be baptized. *Acts 2:38*

- Read your Bible daily. *Joshua 1:9*

- Share your faith. *Mark 16:15*

- Forgive someone. *Ephesians 4:32*

- Teach your children to love God. *Deuteronomy 6:6*

- Other? _____

JOSHUA

Book: 6 of 66

Setting: Moses has died. God's people have been wandering in the desert for 40 years. Moses's assistant Joshua is now the new untested leader.

Author: Joshua

Type of Literature: History. The story of how God fought for His people and got them to their Promised Land.

Date of Writing: 1406-1370 B.C. Joshua writes this book during Israel's war for the Promised Land.

Time Period Covered: 1406-1370 B.C.

Key verses:
Joshua 10:14 ...for the Lord fought for Israel.

Joshua 11:23 So Joshua took control of the entire land, just as the LORD had instructed Moses. He gave it to the people of Israel as their special possession, dividing the land among the tribes. So the land finally had rest from war. (NLT)

BIG IDEA OF JOSHUA:
God fights for His people. He leads us out of our wilderness and into our Promised Land.

3 MAJOR MOMENTS OF JOSHUA:

1. **Battle of Jericho.**

Joshua 6:20 So the people shouted when the priests blew the trumpets. And it happened when the people heard the sound of the trumpet, and the people shouted with a great shout, that the wall fell down flat. Then the people went up into the city, every man straight before him, and they took the city.

2. **The sun stands still.**

Joshua 10:12-14 "Sun, stand still over Gibeon; And Moon, in the Valley of Aijalon." So the sun stood still, And the moon stopped, Till the people had revenge upon their enemies....So the sun stood still in the midst of heaven, and did not hasten to go down for about a whole day. And there has been no day like that, before it or after it, that the LORD heeded the voice of a man; for the LORD fought for Israel.

3. **Joshua's farewell.**

Joshua 24:15 ...if it seems evil to you to serve the LORD, choose for yourselves this day whom you will serve, whether the gods which your fathers served that were on the other side of the River, or the gods of the Amorites, in whose land you dwell. But as for me and my house, we will serve the LORD.

✝ JESUS IN JOSHUA

- **Jesus is our Warrior King. He fights for us!**

Joshua 5:13-15 And it came to pass, when Joshua was by Jericho, that he lifted his eyes and looked, and behold, a Man stood opposite him with His sword drawn in His hand. And Joshua went to Him and said to Him, "Are You for us or for our adversaries?" So He said, "No, but as Commander of the army of the Lord I have now come." And Joshua fell on his face to the earth and worshiped, and said to Him, "What does my Lord say to His servant?" Then the Commander of the LORD's army said to Joshua, "Take your sandal off your foot, for the place where you stand is holy."

Revelation 19:11-16 Now I saw heaven opened, and behold, a white horse. And He who sat on him was called Faithful and True, and in righteousness He judges and makes war. His eyes were like a flame of fire, and on His head were many crowns. He had a name written that no one knew except Himself. He was clothed with a robe dipped in blood, and His name is called The Word of God.

And the armies in heaven, clothed in fine linen, white and clean, followed Him on white horses. Now out of His mouth goes a sharp sword, that with it He should strike the nations. And He Himself will rule them with a rod of iron. He Himself treads the winepress of the fierceness and wrath of Almighty God. And He has on His robe and on His thigh a name written: KING OF KINGS AND LORD OF LORDS.

LET'S APPLY IT!

1. Like God fought for Israel at Jericho, He wants to fight for you. What battle do you need Him to win?

2. God wants to fight for your family and friends as well. Who can you share the gospel with?

3. Like the sun stood still for Joshua, God wants to do miracles for you. What is your sun stand still prayer?

4. Like Joshua asked Israel, "Who will you serve?" God asks you today, "As for you and your house, who will you serve?"

Book: 7 of 66

Author: Anonymous, but many theologians believe it was written by the prophet Samuel.

Type of Literature: History. The book is the story of how Israel forgot God after the death of Joshua and the land descended into chaos, destruction, violence, sin, and death.

Date of Writing: Approx 1043 - 1004 B.C.

Time Period Covered: 1380-1045 B.C. The 350 years of chaos and violence in Israel's history.

12 Judges (deliverers) of Israel:

1. Othniel - *Judges 1:9-21; 3:1-11*
2. Ehud - *Judges 3:12-30*
3. Shamgar - *Judges 3:31-5:6*
4. Deborah/Barak - *Judges 4:1-5:31*
5. Gideon - *Judges 6:1-8:32*
6. Tola - *Judges 10:1-2*
7. Jair - *Judges 10:3-5*
8. Jephthah - *Judges 10:6-12:7*
9. Ibzan - *Judges 12:8-10*
10. Elon - *Judges 12:11-12*
11. Abdon - *Judges 12:13-15*
12. Samson - *Judges 13:1-16:31*

Key verses:

Judges 17:6 ...everyone did what was right in his own eyes.

Judges 21:25 ...everyone did what was right in his own eyes.

BIG IDEA OF JUDGES:
Everyone did what was right in their own eyes.

THE CYCLE
OF SIN IN
JUDGES

SIN, REBELLION
AGAINST GOD

OPPRESSION,
ENSLAVEMENT,
CHAOS, VIOLENCE,
AND DEATH

REPENTANCE

DELIVERER

DELIVERANCE

PEACE

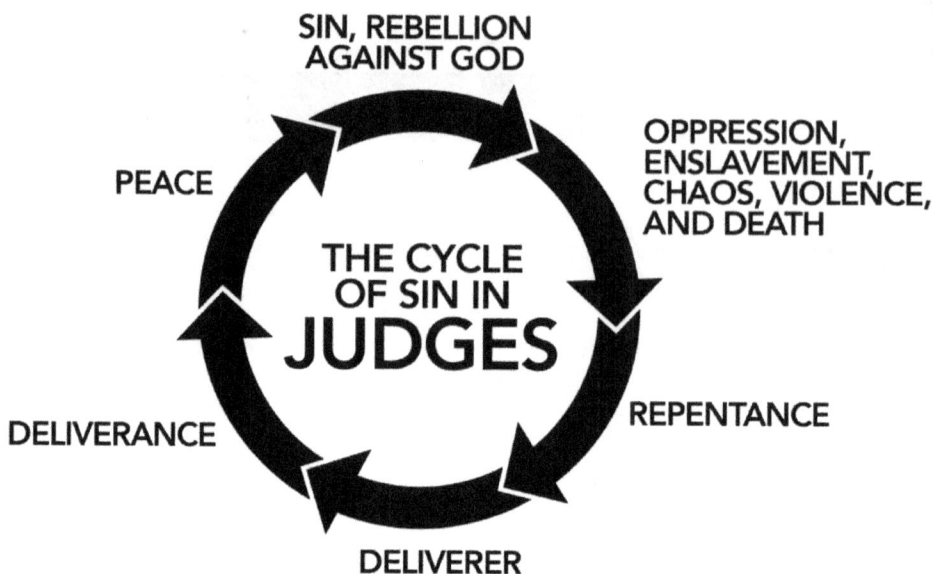

- Sin - Rebellion against God (I will do what is right in my own eyes). The people forget God.

- Oppression/Enslavement/Chaos/Violence/Death - What happens when people do what's right in their own eyes and forget God.

- Repentance - The people hit rock bottom and repent.

- Deliverer - God hear their cries and sends them a Savior/deliverer.

- Deliverance - The people get set free.

- Peace - The people have peace.

✝ JESUS IN JUDGES

- **Jesus is our Deliverer.**

  Judges 3:9 When the children of Israel cried out to the LORD, the LORD raised up a deliverer...

  I Thessalonians 1:10 ...wait for His Son from heaven, whom He raised from the dead, even Jesus who delivers us from the wrath to come.

LET'S APPLY IT!

1. Get off the insanity cycle of sin! Repent and turn to your Deliverer, Jesus!

2. Be someone's deliverer! You are someone's only shot at deliverance from the oppression of sin, Satan, and hell. Who will you seek to save?

RUTH

Book: 8 of 66

Setting: During the time period of the judges, two women move from Moab to Bethlehem in hopes that God would provide for them.

Author: Samuel.

Type of Literature: History. (This is one of the great love stories of the Bible.)

Date of Writing: 1050 B.C.

Time Period Covered: 1160 B.C. - 1100 B.C.

Outline of the Book:

- Ruth 1: Ruth remains loyal to Naomi.
- Ruth 2: Ruth provides for her and Naomi by gleaning from Boaz's field.
- Ruth 3: Ruth asks Boaz to redeem her (marry her).
- Ruth 4: Ruth and Boaz are married. Happily ever after.

Key verses:

Ruth 1:16-17 But Ruth replied, "Don't ask me to leave you and turn back. Wherever you go, I will go; wherever you live, I will live. Your people will be my people, and your God will be my God. Wherever you die, I will die, and there I will be buried. May the LORD punish me severely if I allow anything but death to separate us!" (NLT)

Ruth 4:14 Then the women said to Naomi, "Blessed is the LORD who has not left you without a redeemer today, and may his name become famous in Israel." (NASB)

BIG IDEA OF RUTH:
God is always at work to redeem you and those you love.

4 MAJOR MOMENTS OF RUTH:

1. **Repentance. Elimelech left the Promised Land thinking life is better on the outside. Naomi returns to the Promised Land knowing God will provide.** *Ruth 1:1-5; Ruth 1:6-7*

2. **Faithfulness. Ruth was faithful to Naomi.** *Ruth 1:15-18*

3. **Selflessness. Naomi selflessly plans for Ruth's future.** *Ruth 3:1-3*

4. **Redemption. Boaz lovingly accepted his role as a redeemer.** *Ruth 2:19-20; Ruth 3:11-13*

✝ JESUS IN RUTH

1. **Jesus is our Redeemer.**

   Isaiah 54:4-5 Fear not; you will no longer live in shame. Don't be afraid; there is no more disgrace for you. You will no longer remember the shame of your youth and the sorrows of widowhood. For your Creator will be your husband; the LORD of Heaven's Armies is his name! He is your Redeemer, the Holy One of Israel, the God of all the earth. (NLT)

   Ephesians 1:7 In Him we have redemption through His blood, the forgiveness of sins, according to the riches of His grace.

   Colossians 1:13-14 He has delivered us from the domain of darkness and transferred us to the kingdom of his beloved Son, in whom we have redemption, the forgiveness of sins. (ESV)

2. **Jesus' genealogy.** *(See Matthew 1:1-16)*

LET'S APPLY IT!

REDEMPTION - We are all Naomi and know an outsider like Ruth that needs to be welcomed into the family of God. Who is God calling you to work with and welcome into the family of God?

Book: 9 of 66

Author: Samuel.

Type of Literature: History. This book is the history of Israel's first monarchy. It covers the life of the prophet Samuel, King Saul, and the rise of King David.

Date of Writing: Somewhere between 1105-971 B.C.

Time Period Covered: 1120-1000 B.C.

Key verses: *1 Samuel 8:6-7 ...they said, "Give us a king to judge us." So Samuel prayed to the LORD. And the LORD said to Samuel, "Heed the voice of the people in all that they say to you; for they have not rejected you, but they have rejected Me, that I should not reign over them."*

BIG IDEA OF 1 SAMUEL:
The leadership stories of three great men.

3 MAJOR PLAYERS:

1. **The Prophet Samuel. The theme of his life: listen for the voice of God.**

    I Samuel 3:10 And the LORD came and called as before, "Samuel! Samuel!" And Samuel replied, "Speak, your servant is listening." (NLT)

2. **King Saul. The theme of his life: rebel & miss the blessing.**

    I Samuel 15:22-23 So Samuel said: "Has the LORD as great delight in burnt offerings and sacrifices, As in obeying the voice of the LORD? Behold, to obey is better than sacrifice, And to heed than the fat of rams. For rebellion is as the sin of witchcraft, And stubbornness is as iniquity and idolatry. Because you have rejected the word of the LORD, He also has rejected you from being king."

3. **David. The theme of his life: step up when others step back.**

I Samuel 17:4-11 And a champion went out from the camp of the Philistines, named Goliath, from Gath, whose height was six cubits and a span. He had a bronze helmet on his head, and he was armed with a coat of mail, and the weight of the coat was five thousand shekels of bronze. And he had bronze armor on his legs and a bronze javelin between his shoulders. Now the staff of his spear was like a weaver's beam, and his iron spearhead weighed six hundred shekels; and a shield-bearer went before him. Then he stood and cried out to the armies of Israel, and said to them, "Why have you come out to line up for battle? Am I not a Philistine, and you the servants of Saul? Choose a man for yourselves, and let him come down to me. If he is able to fight with me and kill me, then we will be your servants. But if I prevail against him and kill him, then you shall be our servants and serve us." And the Philistine said, "I defy the armies of Israel this day; give me a man, that we may fight together." When Saul and all Israel heard these words of the Philistine, they were dismayed and greatly afraid.

I Samuel 17:24 ...all the men of Israel, when they saw the man, fled from him and were dreadfully afraid.

I Samuel 17:32 Then David said to Saul, "Let no man's heart fail because of him; your servant will go and fight with this Philistine."

✝ JESUS IN 1 SAMUEL

- **Like David, Jesus stepped up.**

Philippians 2:5-11 You must have the same attitude that Christ Jesus had. Though he was God, he did not think of equality with God as something to cling to. <u>Instead, he gave up his divine privileges; he took the humble position of a slave and was born as a human being. When he appeared in human form, he humbled himself in obedience to God and died a criminal's death on a cross.</u> Therefore, God elevated him to the place of highest honor and gave him the name above all other names, that at the name of Jesus every knee should bow, in heaven and on earth and under the earth, and every tongue declare that Jesus Christ is Lord, to the glory of God the Father.

LET'S APPLY IT!

1. Like God talked to the prophet Samuel, He is talking to you! What is the Spirit of God telling you that you need to do to be used by God?

2. Like King Saul rebelled and missed the blessing, in what area are you rebelling against God and missing His blessing?

3. Like David stepped up rather than stepped back, who do you need to step up for and seek to rescue from the giants of sin, Satan, and hell?

Book: 10 of 66

Author: Probably written by Nathan the prophet or one of his assistants.

Type of Literature: History. This book is the story of King David's rule of Israel.

Date of Writing: Sometime after the death of Solomon (931 B.C.) and before 722 B.C. when the northern kingdom was destroyed.

Time Period Covered: 1011 B.C - 971 B.C. (The rule of King David)

Key verse: *2 Samuel 7:16 ...your house and your kingdom shall be established forever before you. Your throne shall be established forever.*

BIG IDEA OF 2 SAMUEL:
David was both a gracious king and a great failure.

2 MAJOR THEMES OF 2 SAMUEL:

1. **Gracious king. David sought out and welcomed the broken to the king's table.**

   2 Samuel 9:3-7 Then the king said, "Is there not still someone of the house of Saul, to whom I may show the kindness of God?" And Ziba said to the king, "There is still a son of Jonathan who is lame in his feet... Then King David sent and brought him out of the house of Machir the son of Ammiel, from Lo Debar. Now when Mephibosheth the son of Jonathan, the son of Saul, had come to David, he fell on his face and prostrated himself. Then David said, "Mephibosheth?" And he answered, "Here is your servant!" So David said to him, "Do not fear, for I will surely show you kindness for Jonathan your father's sake, and will restore to you all the land of Saul your grandfather; and you shall eat bread at my table continually."

2. **Great failure. David got distracted from his mission by his wealth and power and failed his people.**

2 Samuel 11:1-4 In the spring of the year, <u>when kings normally go out to war, David sent Joab and the Israelite</u> army to fight the Ammonites. They destroyed the Ammonite army and laid siege to the city of Rabbah. However, David stayed behind in Jerusalem. Late one afternoon, after his midday rest, David got out of bed and was walking on the roof of the palace. As he looked out over the city, he noticed a woman of unusual beauty taking a bath. He sent someone to find out who she was, and he was told, "She is Bathsheba, the daughter of Eliam and the wife of Uriah the Hittite." Then David sent messengers to get her; and when she came to the palace, he slept with her. (NLT)

✝ JESUS IN 2 SAMUEL

1. **Like David seeks out and welcomes the broken, Jesus seeks out and welcomes the broken.**

Matthew 9:10-13 Later, Matthew invited Jesus and his disciples to his home as <u>dinner guests</u>, along with <u>many tax collectors and other disreputable sinners</u>. But when the Pharisees saw this, they asked his disciples, "Why does your teacher eat with such scum? When Jesus heard this, he said, "Healthy people don't need a doctor—sick people do." Then he added, "Now go and learn the meaning of this Scripture: 'I want you to show mercy, not offer sacrifices.' For I have come to call not those who think they are righteous, but those who know they are sinners." (NLT)

LET'S APPLY IT!

1. Like David, we must seek out and welcome the broken to the King's table. Who will you invite to the table to feast on the goodness and mercy of God?

2. David got distracted from his mission and failed his people. We must not get distracted from our mission and fail our people. We are the only chance they have!

    We exist to help as many people as we can cross the line of faith and follow Jesus.

Books: 11, 12, 13 & 14 of 66

Author: Jewish tradition says the prophet Jeremiah wrote Kings and the prophet Ezra wrote Chronicles.

Type of Literature: History. 1 & 2 Kings and 1 & 2 Chronicles tell the story of twenty kings of Israel, nineteen kings of Judah, and one queen of Judah.

Time Period Covered: 1000-586 B.C. (David & Solomon's reign to the destruction of Jerusalem.)

Key verses:

I Kings 9:4-7 "...if you will follow me with integrity and godliness, as David your father did, obeying all my commands, decrees, and regulations, then I will establish the throne of your dynasty over Israel forever. For I made this promise to your father, David: 'One of your descendants will always sit on the throne of Israel.' But if you or your descendants abandon me and disobey the commands and decrees I have given you, and if you serve and worship other gods, then I will uproot Israel from this land that I have given them. I will reject this Temple that I have made holy to honor my name. I will make Israel an object of mockery and ridicule among the nations." (NLT)

I Kings 11:6-8 In this way, Solomon did what was evil in the Lord's sight; he refused to follow the Lord completely, as his father, David, had done. On the Mount of Olives, east of Jerusalem, he even built a pagan shrine for Chemosh, the detestable god of Moab, and another for Molech, the detestable god of the Ammonites. Solomon built such shrines for all his foreign wives to use for burning incense and sacrificing to their gods. (NLT)

BIG IDEA OF KINGS & CHRONICLES:
The failure of human kings. We need a better King!

THE KINGS OF ISRAEL & JUDAH:

ISRAEL

Jeroboam I	Jehoahaz	
Nadab	Jehoash	
Baasha	Jeroboam II	
Elah	Zechariah	722
Zimri	Shallum	Exiled to
Omri	Menahem	Assyria
Ahab	Pekahiah	
Ahaziah	Pekah	
Jehoram	Hoshea	
Jehu		

JUDAH

Rehoboam	*Jotham	
Abijah	Ahaz	
*Asa	*Hezekiah	
*Jehoshaphat	Manasseh	586
Jehoram	Amon	Exiled to
Ahaziah	*Josiah	Babylon
Ataliah (Queen)	Jehoahaz	
*Joash	Jehoiakim	
*Amaziah	Jeconiah	
*Uzziah	Zedekiah	

Kings that were good; all others were bad.

✝ JESUS IN KINGS & CHRONICLES

- **Jesus is coming! He is our better King!**

I Chronicles 17:11-14 "...I will raise up one of your descendants, one of your sons, and I will make his kingdom strong... I will secure his throne forever. I will be his father, and he will be my son. I will never take my favor from him... I will confirm him as king over my house and my kingdom for all time, and his throne will be secure forever." (NLT)

Matthew 21:1-9 Now when they drew near Jerusalem, and came to Bethphage, at the Mount of Olives, then Jesus sent two disciples, saying to them, "Go into the village opposite you, and immediately you will find a donkey tied, and a colt with her. Loose them and bring them to Me. And if anyone says anything to you, you shall say, 'The Lord has need of them,' and immediately he will send them... So the disciples went and did as Jesus commanded them. They brought the donkey and the colt, laid their clothes on them, and set Him on them. And a very great multitude spread their clothes on the road; others cut down branches from the trees and spread them on the road. Then the multitudes who went before and those who followed cried out, saying: "Hosanna to the Son of David! 'Blessed is He who comes in the name of the Lord!' Hosanna in the highest!"

LET'S APPLY IT!

- Human kings and all they represent (economies, governments, armies, political, educational & financial systems, etc.) will always fail us! ONLY King Jesus can truly SAVE NOW!

  Romans 8:38-39 For I am persuaded that neither death nor life, nor angels nor principalities nor powers, nor things present nor things to come, nor height nor depth, nor any other created thing, shall be able to separate us from the love of God which is in Christ Jesus our Lord.

- Who will you help to experience the unfailing love of King Jesus?

Book: 15 of 66

Author: Most theologians believe that the Jewish priest, teacher, and scribe Ezra wrote the Book of Ezra.

Type of Literature: History. The Book of Ezra tells the story of the Jewish people returning to Jerusalem following 70 years in Babylonian captivity.

Date of Writing: 460 and 440 B.C.

Time Period Covered: 100 years. 540-440 B.C.

SECTION 1 (EZRA 1-6) BIG IDEA:

- **God's House matters!** In these 6 chapters, the Jews return from Babylonian captivity and focus on rebuilding the temple in Jerusalem. (538-515 B.C.)

Key verses:

Ezra 3:10-11 When the builders laid the foundation of the temple of the LORD, the priests stood in their apparel with trumpets, and the Levites, the sons of Asaph, with cymbals, to praise the LORD, according to the ordinance of David king of Israel. And they sang responsively, praising and giving thanks to the LORD: "For He is good, For His mercy endures forever toward Israel." Then all the people shouted with a great shout, when they praised the LORD, because the foundation of the house of the LORD was laid.

FOCUS ON GOD'S HOUSE

- Attending weekly keeps ourselves and our family connected to God.
- Singing from the heart restores our passion.
- Serving others in our church encourages others in their faith.
- Tithing keeps the mission of God sustainable.
- Studying God's Word with intensity changes our brain and adjusts our character.

- Teaching our children that God matters most sets them up for success.

    Psalms 92:13 Those who are <u>planted in the house</u> of the LORD shall <u>flourish</u> in the courts of our God.

SECTION 2 (Ezra 7-10) BIG IDEA:

- **Holy living matters!** In these 4 chapters, many Israelites (including the leaders) have married unbelievers and drifted into dysfunctional, unholy living. Ezra loses his mind with frustration. This was the same rebellion that got them destroyed and exiled in the first place!

⚷ Key verses:
Ezra 9:3-6 So when I heard this thing, I tore my garment and my robe, and plucked out some of the hair of my head and beard, and sat down astonished... I fell on my knees and spread out my hands to the LORD my God. And I said: "O my God, I am too ashamed and humiliated to lift up my face to You, my God; for our iniquities have risen higher than our heads, and our guilt has grown up to the heavens.

Ezra 9:11-12 'The land which you are entering to possess is an unclean land, with the uncleanness of the peoples of the lands, with their abominations which have filled it from one end to another with their impurity. Now therefore, <u>do not give your daughters as wives for their sons, nor take their daughters to your sons</u>; ...that you may be strong and eat the good of the land, and leave it as an inheritance to your children forever.'

2 Corinthians 6:14 Do not be unequally yoked together with unbelievers. For what fellowship has righteousness with lawlessness? And what communion has light with darkness?

✝ JESUS IN EZRA

1. Both Ezra & Jesus focus on God's House.

Matthew 16:18 ...I will build my church, and the gates of hell will not prevail against it. (BSB)

2. Both Ezra & Jesus were brokenhearted over the dysfunctional lives of their people.

Luke 19:41 ...when he drew near and saw the city, he wept over it... (ESV)

LET'S APPLY IT!

1. If you are living a dysfunctional unholy life: REPENT!

I John 1:9 If we confess our sins, He is faithful and just to forgive us our sins and cleanse us from all unrighteousness.

2. If you have drifted from your focus on God's House: RE-FOCUS!

Hebrews 10:25 ...let us not neglect our meeting together, as some people do, but encourage one another, especially now that the day of his return is drawing near. (NLT)

3. If you have compromised with sin or with unbelievers: RUN.

2 Timothy 2:22 Run from anything that stimulates youthful lusts. Instead, pursue righteous living, faithfulness, love, and peace. Enjoy the companionship of those who call on the Lord with pure hearts. (NLT)

NEHEMIAH

Book: 16 of 66

Author: Jewish tradition identifies Nehemiah as the author. Much of the book is written from his first-person perspective.

Type of Literature: History. The Book of Nehemiah is the sequel to the Book of Ezra and tells the story of Nehemiah leading his people to rebuild the walls of Jerusalem.

Date of Writing: 445-420 B.C.

Time Period Covered: 444-430 B.C.

BIG IDEA OF NEHEMIAH:
Leadership strategies to advance God's Kingdom.

Key Verses:

Nehemiah 1:1-4a It came to pass in the month of Chislev, in the twentieth year, as I was in Shushan the citadel, that Hanani one of my brethren came with men from Judah; and I asked them concerning the Jews who had escaped, who had survived the captivity, and concerning Jerusalem. And they said to me, "The survivors who are left from the captivity in the province are there in great distress and reproach. The wall of Jerusalem is also broken down, and its gates are burned with fire." So it was, when I heard these words, that I sat down and wept, and mourned for many days...

1. **Embrace your holy discontent.**

Nehemiah 1:4b I was fasting and praying before the God of heaven.

2. **Pray and fast until God gives you an action plan.**

Nehemiah 2:1-5 And it came to pass in the month of Nisan, in the twentieth year of King Artaxerxes, when wine was before him, that I took the wine and gave it to the king. Now I had never been sad in his presence before. Therefore the king said to me, "Why is your face sad, since you are not sick? This is nothing but sorrow of heart." So I became dreadfully afraid, and said to the king, "May the king live forever! Why should my face not be sad, when the city, the place of my fathers' tombs, lies waste, and its gates are burned with fire?" Then the king said to me, "What do you request?" So I prayed to the God of heaven. And I said to the king, "If it pleases the king, and if your servant has found favor in your sight, I ask that you send me to Judah, to the city of my fathers' tombs, that I may rebuild it."

3. Take a risk! Boldly step in faith in the direction God wants you to go!

Nehemiah 4:17 The laborers carried on their work with one hand supporting their load and one hand holding a weapon. (NLT)

4. Don't quit! Keep resolutely moving forward to advance God's Kingdom!

Brutiful:
- Beautiful - We want to celebrate as the lost cross the line of faith.
- Brutal - We are willing to pay the price for the cause of Christ.

✝ JESUS IN NEHEMIAH

1. Jesus, like Nehemiah, had a holy discontent.

John 3:16 <u>For God so loved the world</u> that He gave His one and only Son that whoever believes in Him shall not perish but have eternal life. (NIV)

2. **Jesus, like Nehemiah, was willing to do whatever it takes to complete the mission.**

Luke 9:51 ...Jesus resolutely set out for Jerusalem. (NIV)

LET'S APPLY IT!

1. What is your God-given holy discontent?

2. Are you/will you pray and fast and ask God for a plan of action?

3. What risk/step of faith is God asking you take?

4. Are you willing to pay the price for the cause of Christ?

   Acts 15:26 ...[these are the] men who have risked their lives for the name of our Lord Jesus Christ.

ESTHER

Book: 17 of 66

Author: The author of Esther is anonymous, though it is obviously somebody familiar with the characters of the story. Many believe it was a friend of Mordecai, Esther's uncle.

Type of Literature: History. The story of how a Jewish girl saves God's people from a holocaust.

Date of Writing: Between 470 B.C. and 424 B.C.

Time Period Covered: A 10-year period between 483 B.C. - 473 B.C.

Basics of the story:

- A young Jewish girl named Hadassah is kidnapped by the royal guards and forced to compete for the affection of the king.
- Whoever wins the king's lusty contest gets to be the new queen.
- Hadassah wins and her name is changed to Esther meaning "star".
- Esther uses her new position of influence to stop an evil man named Haman from committing a holocaust against the Jews.
- Haman is executed and the Jews are saved.

Key verse:
Esther 4:14 "...who knows whether you have come to the kingdom for such a time as this?"

BIG IDEA OF ESTHER:
God puts us in situations to save the lives of others!

Two important theological concepts we learn in Esther:

1. **Sovereignty - God is in charge and working behind the scenes for your good!**

    -   In Esther, God's name is never mentioned!

    -   That does not mean God was not at work! Even when you can't see Him, He is still on the throne working for your good.

    -   His sovereign plan put Esther in her role to save His people!

        Romans 8:28 ...we know that God causes everything to work together for the good of those who love God and are called according to his purpose for them. (NLT)

2. **Grace: God uses the available, not the perfect.**

    -   Esther had a messy/broken life, yet God still used her. (She won a sex contest to be crowned queen.)

        Esther 2:14 In the evening she went, and in the morning she returned to the second house of the women, to the custody of Shaashgaz, the king's eunuch who kept the concubines. She would not go in to the king again unless the king delighted in her and called for her by name.

    -   God does not call the qualified. He qualifies the called!

✝ JESUS IN ESTHER

-   **Like Esther rescued her people from earthly destruction, Jesus rescues us from eternal destruction.**

    I Thessalonians 1:10 ...wait for His Son from heaven, whom He raised from the dead, even <u>Jesus who delivers us from the wrath to come</u>.

Matthew 25:46 ...they [those who reject Christ] will go away into eternal punishment, but the righteous [in Christ] will go into eternal life. (NLT)

LET'S APPLY IT!

1. God is on the throne and at work behind the scenes! Don't stop trusting Him!

2. You are in your situation to rescue those around you. Use your influence to save someone else!

3. You are not too broken to be used by God! His grace is greater than your sin, shame, and pain (and even your excuses)!

JOB

Author: The author of Job is unknown. Written by someone who was an eyewitness to the events and conversations recorded in the book.

Type of Literature: History. Job is the story of Satan's attack against him and how he keeps his faith through pain and adversity.

Date of Writing: Oldest book in the Bible. Written before Genesis. Approximately 2100 to 1900 B.C.

Time Period Covered: No time period is recorded. Job probably lived during or before Abraham.

BIG IDEA OF JOB:
There is a spiritual and physical side of adversity.

THE SPIRITUAL REALM:

Job 1:1 There was a man in the land of Uz, whose name was Job; and that man was blameless and upright, and one who feared God and shunned evil.

Job 1:6-11 Now there was a day when the sons of God came to present themselves before the LORD, and Satan also came among them. And the LORD said to Satan, "From where do you come?" So Satan answered the LORD and said, "From going to and fro on the earth, and from walking back and forth on it." Then the LORD said to Satan, "Have you considered My servant Job, that there is none like him on the earth, a blameless and upright man, one who fears God and shuns evil?" So Satan answered the LORD and said, "Does Job fear God for nothing? Have You not made a hedge around him, around his household, and around all that he has on every side? You have blessed the work of his hands, and his possessions have increased in the land. But now, stretch out Your hand and touch all that he has, and he will surely curse You to Your face!"

1. **Satan must get permission to mess with God's people.**

   Job 1:12 ...the LORD said to Satan, "Behold, all that he has is in your power..."

   Job 2:6 ...the LORD said to Satan, "Behold, he is in your hand, but spare his life."

2. **If God gives permission, God believes we can handle it.**

3. **The enemy attacks:**

   - Satan put the idea in bad guys' heads to steal Job's stuff & murder Job's employees. *(vs. 1:13-15)*

   - Satan drops fire from heaven. *(vs. 1:16)*

   - Satan again puts the idea in bad guys' heads to steal Job's stuff & murder Job's employees. *(vs. 1:17)*

   - Satan manipulates the weather (windstorm) and kills Job's family in a "natural disaster". *(vs. 1:18-19)*

   - Satan gives Job a disease. *(vs. 2:7)*

THE PHYSICAL REALM:

🔑 Key Verses of Job:

Job 1:20-21 Then Job arose, tore his robe, and shaved his head; and he fell to the ground and worshiped. And he said: "Naked I came from my mother's womb, And naked shall I return there. The LORD gave, and the LORD has taken away; Blessed be the name of the LORD."

Job 2:10 ..."Shall we indeed accept good from God, and shall we not accept adversity?" In all this Job did not sin with his lips.

1. **Job keeps his faith in God despite his pain and suffering.**

2. **Job discusses with four friends & God WHY there is pain and suffering.** *(Chapters 3-41)*

Job 42:10,12 …the LORD restored Job's losses… Indeed the LORD gave Job twice as much as he had before. …the LORD blessed the latter days of Job more than his beginning…

3. **God gives Job double for his trouble.**

✝ JESUS IN JOB

- Like Job, Jesus is attacked multiple times by Satan and overcomes.
- Satan tries & fails to kill Jesus at his birth. *Matthew 2:16-18; Revelation 12:4*
- Jesus defeats Satan in the wilderness temptation. *Matthew 4*
- Jesus triumphs over Satan at the cross.

  Colossians 2:15 [Jesus] disarmed the spiritual rulers and authorities. He shamed them publicly by his victory over them on the cross. (NLT)

LET'S APPLY IT!

1. God is so much greater than Satan. Satan can't touch you without God's permission. (Pray for you and your families' protection.)

    Job 1:10 Have You not made a hedge around him, around his household, and around all that he has on every side?…

2. When you go through hard things, know that God believes in you.

3. Don't foolishly underestimate Satan! His power is real.

    I Peter 5:8 Stay alert! Watch out for your great enemy, the devil. He prowls around like a roaring lion, looking for someone to devour. (NLT)

Ephesians 6:12 For we are not fighting against flesh-and-blood enemies, but against evil rulers and authorities of the unseen world, against mighty powers in this dark world, and against evil spirits in the heavenly places. (NLT)

4. Don't lose your faith during adversity. God blesses those who persevere.

   James 1:12 <u>Blessed</u> is the man who remains <u>steadfast</u> under trial, for when he has stood the test he will receive the crown of life, which God has promised to those who love him. (ESV)

Book: 19 of 66

Author: Psalms was written by multiple authors and collected over many generations of God-followers.

- Moses wrote Psalm 90.
- David was responsible for 73.
- Asaph wrote 12.
- The descendants of Korah wrote 10.
- Solomon wrote 1 or maybe 2.
- Ethan & Heman are responsible for 2.
- The remaining Psalms are anonymous.

Type of Literature: Poetry. The book was originally titled *Tehillim* which means "praise songs" in Hebrew. The English title of *Psalms* means "sacred songs or hymns."

Date of Writing: Psalms was written and collected over a 1,000-year period. Moses wrote around 1400 B.C. David wrote around 1000 B.C and in the time of Ezra (450 B.C.) the final collection was completed and organized.

BIG IDEA OF PSALMS:
Worship God for WHO He is and WHAT He has done.
Psalms is the "Song Book of Faith".

Different Psalms were written to communicate different emotions regarding the writer's situation.

Some categories of Psalms:

- Lament Psalms - Crying out to God for help in difficult circumstances (Psalms 130)

- Adoration Psalms - Adoration of God for His greatness or goodness (Psalms 145)

- Thanksgiving Psalms - Gratitude for deliverance or provision from God (Psalms 100)

- Victory Psalms - Celebration that God has overcome our enemies (Psalms 44)

- Pilgrim Psalms - Joy for being able to go to Jerusalem and worship (Psalms 84)

✝ JESUS IN PSALMS

1. Jesus is our Creator.

Psalms 19:1 The heavens proclaim the glory of God. The skies display his craftsmanship. (NLT)

Psalms 139:13-17 You made all the delicate, inner parts of my body and knit me together in my mother's womb. Thank you for making me so wonderfully complex! Your workmanship is marvelous—how well I know it. You watched me as I was being formed in utter seclusion, as I was woven together in the dark of the womb. You saw me before I was born. Every day of my life was recorded in your book. Every moment was laid out before a single day had passed. How precious are your thoughts about me, O God. They cannot be numbered! (NLT)

2. Jesus is our Rescuer.

Psalms 34:18 The LORD is close to the brokenhearted; he rescues those whose spirits are crushed. (NLT)

Psalms 68:20 Our God is a God who saves! The Sovereign LORD rescues us from death. (NLT)

3. Jesus is our Forgiver.

Psalms 32:5 ...I confessed all my sins to you and stopped trying to hide my guilt. I said to myself, "I will confess my rebellion to the LORD." And you forgave me! All my guilt is gone. (NLT)

Psalms 86:15 But you, O Lord, are a God of compassion and mercy, slow to get angry and filled with unfailing love and faithfulness.

Psalms 103:12 He has removed our sins as far from us as the east is from the west. (NLT)

4. Jesus is our Provider.

Psalms 23:1-3 The Lord is my shepherd; I shall not want. He makes me to lie down in green pastures; He leads me beside the still waters. He restores my soul...

Psalms 103:2-5 Bless the LORD, O my soul, And forget not all His benefits: Who forgives all your iniquities, Who heals all your diseases, Who redeems your life from destruction, Who crowns you with lovingkindness and tender mercies, Who satisfies your mouth with good things, So that your youth is renewed like the eagle's.

5. Jesus is our hope and peace.

Psalms 46:1-3,10 God is our refuge and strength, A very present help in trouble. Therefore we will not fear, Even though the earth be removed, And though the mountains be carried into the midst of the sea; Though its waters roar and be troubled, Though the mountains shake with its swelling... Be still, and know that I am God; I will be exalted among the nations, I will be exalted in the earth.

Psalms 43:5 Why are you cast down, O my soul? And why are you disquieted within me? Hope in God; For I shall yet praise Him, The help of my countenance and my God.

LET'S APPLY IT!

1. Express your emotions to God! He wants a relationship with the real you!

2. This week read the Psalms every day and ask yourself, "What is the writer feeling?" Express your emotions to God in prayer, writing or a song.

3. Turn off secular music & spend the week ONLY listening to worship music. These modern Psalms will grow your faith and put peace in your heart.

Book: 20 of 66

Author: King Solomon, the son of King David, is the primary author of Proverbs.

Type of Literature: Wisdom. Proverbs is short "fortune cookie" truths from God to help us make wise choices.

Date of Writing: Though Solomon is the primary author, the book's final compilation was completed around the time of King Hezekiah, putting the date of writing between 970-697 B.C.

BIG IDEA OF PROVERBS:
Wisdom! This book is designed to get us to value God's wisdom and use it in all areas of life.

Key Verse:
Proverbs 4:7 Wisdom is the principal thing; Therefore, get wisdom. And in all your getting, get understanding.

Same verse in the NIV translation:
Proverbs 4:7 The beginning of wisdom is this: Get wisdom. Though it cost all you have, get understanding.

HOW TO GET WISDOM

1. Make the Bible your source for ultimate truth.

Proverbs 2:6-7 For the LORD gives wisdom; From His mouth come knowledge and understanding; He stores up sound wisdom for the upright…

Proverbs 3:5-8 Trust in the LORD with all your heart, And lean not on your own understanding; In all your ways acknowledge Him, And He shall direct your paths. Do not be wise in your own eyes; Fear the LORD and depart from evil. It will be health to your flesh, and strength to your bones.

2. Learn what the Bible actually says and means.

Proverbs 19:2 It is not good to have zeal without knowledge, nor to be hasty and miss the way. (NIV 1984)

3. Use the wealth of wisdom in your daily life.

Examples:
a. Friendships – *Proverbs 13:20*
b. Words – *Proverbs 18:21; Proverbs 10:19*
c. Finances – *Proverbs 3:9-10*
d. Conflict – *Proverbs 15:1*
e. Mind your own business – *Proverbs 26:17*
f. Parenting – *Proverbs 19:18; Proverbs 22:6*
g. Releasing control – *Proverbs 19:21*
h. Workday – *Proverbs 16:3*
i. Business – *Proverbs 27:23-24*

✝ JESUS IN PROVERBS

- **Jesus is the source of all wisdom and our example for living out God's best for our life.**

  1 Corinthians 1:30 But of Him you are in Christ Jesus, who became for us wisdom from God...

  Colossians 2:3 ...Christ, in whom are hidden <u>all</u> the treasures of <u>wisdom and knowledge</u>.

LET'S APPLY IT!

1. Trust that God's wisdom works & just do it.

   Proverbs 1:7 The fear of the LORD is the beginning of knowledge, but fools despise wisdom and instruction.

   James 4:17 Therefore, to him who knows to do good and does not do it, to him it is sin.

2. Be willing to receive coaching and make corrections.

   Proverbs 19:20 Listen to advice and accept discipline, and at the end you will be counted among the wise. (NIV)

3. Make a plan to GET MORE WISDOM!

   Proverbs 4:7 ...Get wisdom. Though it cost all you have, get understanding. (NIV)

   a. Set a time to read Scripture daily so you actually know God's truth.

   b. Learn how to understand the Bible and apply it to your life.

   c. Find wise people to learn from.

Book: 21 of 66

Author: The author identifies himself by the title of *qoheleth* (Hebrew), which means "preacher" (1:1). Jewish and Christian theologians & tradition point to King Solomon as the "preacher".

Type of Literature: Wisdom. The writer is exploring the meaning of life.

Date of Writing: Written sometime before Solomon's death in 931 B.C.

BIG IDEA OF ECCLESIASTES:
What is the purpose or meaning of life IF there is no God?

Ecclesiastes 1:2 "Everything is meaningless," says the Teacher, "completely meaningless!" (NLT)

IF THERE IS NO GOD...
Ecclesiastes 10:19 A feast is made for laughter, And wine makes merry; But money answers everything.

Key verses: In twelve chapters, Solomon explores and indulges in all the things people live for to see if there is any real meaning in any of it.

1. **Brainiac Life: knowledge & non-biblical learning.**

   Ecclesiastes 1:16-18; Ecclesiastes 2:14-16

2. **Party Life: pleasure.**

   Ecclesiastes 2:1-3

3. **Playboy Life: wealth & sex.**

   Ecclesiastes 2:4-11

4. **CEO Life: work & success.**

   Ecclesiastes 2:18-23

5. **Power Life: popularity & political victories.**

   Ecclesiastes 4:13-16

6. **His Conclusion: Life only has meaning if we live in light of eternity.**

   Ecclesiastes 12:13-14 Let us hear the conclusion of the whole matter: Fear God and keep His commandments, For this is man's all. For God will bring every work into judgment, Including every secret thing, Whether good or evil.

✝ JESUS IN ECCLESIASTES

- **Jesus rescues us from a meaningless life!**

  Matthew 16:26 ...what do you benefit if you gain the whole world but lose your own soul?... (NLT)

  John 10:10 ..."I have come so that they would have LIFE and have it to the FULL." (NIV)

LET'S APPLY IT!

- **Life is short, eternity is long. Live for Jesus!**

  "Only one life, yes only one, Soon will its fleeting hours be done; Then, in 'that day' my Lord to meet, And stand before His judgment seat; Only one life, 'twill soon be past, Only what's done for Christ will last."

  - C.T. Studd

  Colossians 3:17 ...whatever you do in word or deed, do all in the name of the Lord Jesus...

SONG OF SONGS/SOLOMON

📖 **Title:** Solomon wrote 1,005 songs (1 Kings 4:32), but this was His best–the Song of Songs.

📑 **Book:** 22 of 66

👤 **Author:** King Solomon is the writer. He is specifically named 7 times either as an author (1:1) or as a major character (1:5; 3:7, 9, 11; 8:11, 12).

📝 **Type of Literature:** Poetry. The book is a poem about romance, marriage, love, and sex within the context of marriage.

📅 **Date of Writing:** Song of Solomon was written during King Solomon's reign between 970–931 B.C.

👥 **Audience:** This book was written mostly for engaged couples as a pre-marital counseling "study guide" to get ready for marriage.

BIG IDEA OF SONG OF SOLOMON:
God blesses His people with the gifts of romance, marriage, love, and sex.

This book combats two foolish extremes:

1. **Asceticism - the denial of all pleasure.**

    Song of Solomon 5:1 Eat, friends, and drink; drink your fill of love. (NIV)

    I Timothy 6:17 ...put their hope in God, who richly provides us with everything for our enjoyment. (NIV)

2. **Hedonism - the pursuit of only pleasure.**

    Song of Solomon 3:5 Promise me, O women of Jerusalem, by the gazelles and wild deer, not to awaken love until the time is right. (NLT)

    I Corinthians 6:18 Flee sexual immorality. Every sin that a man does is outside the body, but he who commits sexual immorality sins against his own body.

🔑 Key Verses:

- **Romance:** *Song of Solomon 1:15; 1:2; 7:10*

- **Marriage:** *Song of Solomon 4:9; Proverbs 18:22*

- **Love:** *Song of Solomon 8:6; I Corinthians 13:8*

- **Sex:** *Song of Solomon 4:4-7; 11-16; I Corinthians 7:3-5*

✝ JESUS IN SONG OF SOLOMON

- **Song of Songs (in a loose sense) can be interpreted as how much Christ loves us.**

  Song of Solomon 2:4 ...His banner over me is love. (NASB)

  Romans 8:38-39 For I am persuaded that neither death nor life, nor angels nor principalities nor powers, nor things present nor things to come, nor height nor depth, nor any other created thing, shall be able to separate us from the love of God which is in Christ Jesus our Lord.

LET'S APPLY IT!

1. Honor God with love, sex, romance, and marriage - whether you are married or single.

   Hebrews 13:4 Marriage should be honored by all, and the marriage bed kept pure, for God will judge the adulterer and all the sexually immoral. (NIV)

2. Remember your spouse is a treasure. Treat them that way! Words, romance, attention, time, etc.

3. Enjoy sex in the context of marriage. Do not neglect this important part of your marriage.

ISAIAH

Book: 23 of 66

Author: The prophet/preacher Isaiah is the writer.

Type of Literature: Sermon/prophecy. Isaiah is warning the people of Israel to turn back to God, predicting coming judgment, and the crucifixion, resurrection, and reign of Christ.

Audience: Isaiah preached to the people of Judah and Jerusalem. (Isaiah 1:1)

Date of Writing: Approximately 650 B.C. Jewish tradition says that Isaiah was killed during the reign of evil King Manasseh (695-642 B.C.). So the book would have been completed no later than 642 B.C.

Time Period Covered: Approximately 740-650 B.C. Isaiah preached during the reigns of kings Uzziah, Jotham & Hezekiah, who did what was right in the eyes of the Lord (2 Chronicles 26:4, 27:2, 29:2). And then King Ahaz was an evil king who burned his son alive as an offering to demons (2 Kings 16:3-4), and lastly Manasseh, who was evil and had Isaiah placed in a hollow log and sawn in half.

BIG IDEA OF ISAIAH:
The Gospel!

Isaiah is a mini-Bible. It is 66 chapters like the Bible is 66 books. It is referred to as the "5th Gospel" because more than any other book in the Old Testament, it clearly explains repentance, salvation, Jesus' birth, death, and resurrection, heaven and hell, and the future reign of Christ.

THE GOSPEL IN ISAIAH:

1. God is holy & His people are not.

Isaiah 6:3; Isaiah 64:6

2. **God can't be holy or good if He does not punish sin.**

   Isaiah 13:11; Isaiah 1:31

3. **God gives grace to sinners who repent.**

   Isaiah 30:15; Isaiah 1:18; Isaiah 43:25

✝ KEY VERSES & JESUS IN ISAIAH

1. Jesus came to Earth to save us! ↘

Isaiah 7:14 Therefore the Lord himself will give you a sign. Behold, the virgin shall conceive and bear a son, and shall call his name Immanuel.

Isaiah 9:6 For to us a child is born, to us a son is given; and the government shall be upon his shoulder, and his name shall be called Wonderful Counselor, Mighty God, Everlasting Father, Prince of Peace. (ESV)

2. Jesus died to pay the price for our sins! ✝

Isaiah 53:5-6 ...he was pierced for our rebellion, crushed for our sins. He was beaten so we could be whole. He was whipped so we could be healed. All of us, like sheep, have strayed away. We have left God's paths to follow our own. Yet the Lord laid on him the sins of us all. (NLT)

3. Jesus rose to give us new life! ⌒

Isaiah 53:9-11 ...he was buried like a criminal; he was put in a rich man's grave. But it was the LORD's good plan to crush him and cause him grief. Yet when his life is made an offering for sin, he will have many descendants. He will enjoy a long life, and the LORD's good plan will prosper in his hands. When he sees all that is accomplished by his anguish, he will be satisfied. And because of his experience, my righteous servant will make it possible for many to be counted righteous... (NLT)

4. Jesus left to prepare a place for us! ⬈

Isaiah 25:6-9 ...the LORD of Heaven's Armies will spread a wonderful feast for all the people of the world. It will be a delicious banquet with clear, well-aged wine and choice meat. There he will remove the cloud of gloom, the shadow of death that hangs over the earth. He will swallow up death forever! The Sovereign LORD will wipe away all tears. He will remove forever all insults and mockery against his land and people. The LORD has spoken! In that day the people will proclaim, "This our God! We trusted in him, and he saved us! This is the LORD, in whom we trusted. Let us rejoice in the salvation he brings!" (NLT)

5. Jesus will return to fix the world! ⬊

Isaiah 11:4-10 ...The earth will shake at the force of his word, and one breath from his mouth will destroy the wicked. He will wear righteousness like a belt and truth like an undergarment. In that day the wolf and the lamb will live together; the leopard will lie down with the baby goat. The calf and the yearling will be safe with the lion, and a little child will lead them all. The cow will graze near the bear. The cub and the calf will lie down together. The lion will eat hay like a cow. The baby will play safely near the hole of a cobra. Yes, a little child will put its hand in a nest of deadly snakes without harm. Nothing will hurt or destroy in all my holy mountain, for as the waters fill the sea, so the earth will be filled with people who know the LORD. In that day the heir to David's throne will be a banner of salvation to all the world... (NLT)

LET'S APPLY IT!

Acts 16:31-33 ..."Believe on the Lord Jesus Christ, and you will be saved, you and your household." Then they spoke the word of the Lord to him and to all who were in his house... And immediately he and all his family were baptized.

JEREMIAH & LAMENTATIONS

Books: 24 & 25 of 66

Author: Originally Jeremiah & Lamentations were one book. Jeremiah the prophet is the writer of both. He is known as the "weeping prophet" because he was brokenhearted over his people's sin and coming judgment. Jeremiah never married or had children because God said the land was destined for destruction. (Jeremiah 16:1-4)

Type of Literature: Sermon/prophecy. The Book of Jeremiah is the final prophecies to Judah/Jerusalem warning of coming destruction if the nation does not repent. Lamentations is a "lament" (brokenhearted cry to God) because Jeremiah has witnessed the destruction of Judah exactly as he predicted.

Audience: Jeremiah preached to the people of Judah/Jerusalem before and after their destruction. The audience reacted to his preaching by persecuting him with mocking, threats, and torture. There were only two recorded converts during his ministry. Extra biblical sources suggest that he was stoned to death because he was hated so much.

Date of Writing: Between 630 and 580 B.C.

Time Period Covered: 630 - 580 B.C. The writing covers the reign of five Jewish Kings (Josiah, Jehoahaz, Jehoiakim, Jehoiachin and Zedekiah). It also covers the rise of Babylonian king Nebuchadnezzar who marched on Jerusalem, killed the people, destroyed the city and the temple (586 B.C.), and deported & enslaved those left alive back to Babylon.

BIG IDEA OF JEREMIAH & LAMENTATIONS:
Turn from your rebellion back to (YHWH/Jehovah) or suffer the consequences of sin.

How was Judah living in rebellion to God? They had rejected worship of Jehovah & were worshipping 3 demon gods:

1. **Baal - demon god of prosperity and money. Often represented as a bull.**

    - We worship this same demonic idol when we choose money/prosperity over Christ.

    Matthew 6:24 "No one can serve two masters. For you will hate one and love the other; you will be devoted to one and despise the other. You cannot serve God and be enslaved to money." (NLT)

2. **Molech - demon god of fire and power. He was worshipped by child sacrifice.**

    - We worship this same demon when we choose abortion over lovingly raising children.

    Psalms 106:36-38 They served their idols, Which became a snare to them. They even sacrificed their sons And their daughters to demons, And shed innocent blood, The blood of their sons and daughters, Whom they sacrificed to the idols of Canaan; And the land was polluted with blood.

3. **Asherah - demon god of sex. She was worshipped with sex acts under the asherah pole.**

    - We worship this same demonic idol when we choose sexual immorality over Christ.

    I Corinthians 6:18-20 Run from sexual sin! No other sin so clearly affects the body as this one does. For sexual immorality is a sin against your own body. Don't you realize that your body is the temple of the Holy Spirit, who lives in you and was given to you by God? You do not belong to yourself, for God bought you with a high price. So you must honor God with your body. (NLT)

🔑 Key Verses:

- God's heart.

  Jeremiah 31:3; Jeremiah 29:11

- The people's rebellion.

  Jeremiah 16:10-11; Jeremiah 32:29

- Sin's price tag.

  Jeremiah 52:12-13; Lamentations 2:11

✝ JESUS IN JEREMIAH & LAMENTATIONS

- **The new covenant prophesied.**

  Jeremiah 31:31-34 "The day is coming," says the LORD, "when I will make a new covenant with the people of Israel and Judah. …this is the new covenant I will make with the people of Israel after those days," says the LORD. "I will put my instructions deep within them, and I will write them on their hearts. I will be their God, and they will be my people. And they will not need to teach their neighbors, nor will they need to teach their relatives, saying, 'You should know the LORD.' For everyone, from the least to the greatest, will know me already," says the LORD. "And I will forgive their wickedness, and I will never again remember their sins." (NLT)

  Luke 22:20 After supper he took another cup of wine and said, "This cup is the new covenant between God and his people—an agreement confirmed with my blood, which is poured out as a sacrifice for you." (NLT)

LET'S APPLY IT!

1. Repent! Turn from the 3 demon gods that got Judah destroyed and worship Jesus alone!

    *   Money (Baal)
    *   Selfishness (Molech)
    *   Sexual misconduct (Asherah)

    Jeremiah 4:1 "...if you wanted to return to me, you could. You could throw away your detestable idols and stray away no more." (NLT)

2. Receive! God has grace and mercy through the new covenant!

    Lamentations 3:22-25 Through the LORD's mercies we are not consumed, Because His compassions fail not. They are new every morning; Great is Your faithfulness. "The LORD is my portion," says my soul, "Therefore I hope in Him!" The LORD is good to those who wait for Him, To the soul who seeks Him.

3. Relationship! Stay close to Jesus and He will walk with you and guide your life.

    Jeremiah 33:3 "Call to Me, and I will answer you, and show you great and mighty things, which you do not know."

Book: 26 of 66

Author: The prophet/priest Ezekiel is the author. (Ezekiel 1:3). He lived during the same time period as Jeremiah & Daniel. Like Daniel, he was eventually exiled to Babylon.

Type of Literature: Sermon/prophecy.

- Prophecy of Jerusalem's ruin & the Jews scattered among the nations (1-24)
- Prophecy of God's judgment on the Jews' enemies (25-32)
- A call to repentance (33)
- Israel's future restoration and return (34-48)

Audience: This book was written to the Jews living in exile in Babylon. Many still lived in rebellion against God even though they had witnessed the destruction of Jerusalem. Others needed encouragement as they waited to see God work miracles like He had in the past.

Date of Writing: 592 to 570 B.C. Ezekiel wrote before, during, and after the Babylonian destruction of Jerusalem in 586 B.C.

BIG IDEA OF EZEKIEL:
"God's Resurrecting Grace": If you will turn back to God, He will give you a new heart and resurrect your life.

Key Verses:

1. Turn back to God and live!

Ezekiel 33:10-11 "…our transgressions and our sins lie upon us, and we pine away in them, how can we then live?" "Say to them: 'As I live,' says the Lord God, 'I have no pleasure in the death of the wicked, but that the wicked turn from his way and live…'"

John 10:10 "I have come that they may have LIFE, and have it to the FULL." (NIV)

2. God wants to give you a heart transplant!

Ezekiel 36:26-27 "I will give you a new heart and put a new spirit within you; I will take the heart of stone out of your flesh and give you a heart of flesh. I will put My Spirit within you and cause you to walk in My statutes, and you will keep My judgments and do them."

3. God will bring your "dry bones" to life through His Word and His Spirit.

Ezekiel 37:1-2 The hand of the LORD came upon me and brought me out in the Spirit of the LORD, and set me down in the midst of the valley; and it was full of bones.

- This is what all of us are like without Christ:

"We are DEAD in our trespasses and sins." (Ephesians 2:1)

Ezekiel 37:3-8a …And He said to me, "Son of man, can these bones live?" So I answered, "O Lord God, You know." Again He said to me, "Prophesy to these bones, and say to them, 'O dry bones, hear the WORD of the Lord!'" …So I prophesied as I was commanded; and as I prophesied, there was a noise, and suddenly a rattling; and the bones came together, bone to bone. Indeed, as I looked, the sinews and the flesh came upon them, and the skin covered them over…

- His Word is what will put your life back together!

Ezekiel 37:8b-10 …but there was no breath in them. Also He said to me, "Prophesy to the breath, prophesy, son of man, and say to the breath, 'Thus says the Lord God: Come from the four winds, O breath, and breathe on these slain, that they may live.'" So I prophesied as He commanded me, and breath came into them, and they lived, and stood upon their feet, an exceedingly great army.

- His Spirit is spiritual breath! You need the Word & Holy Spirit to truly live!

Romans 8:6 ...the mind governed by the Spirit is LIFE...

✝ JESUS IN EZEKIEL

- **Jesus is the Good Shepherd.**

Ezekiel 34:12; 16 I will be like a shepherd looking for his scattered flock. I will find my sheep and rescue them from all the places where they were scattered... I will search for my lost ones who strayed away, and I will bring them safely home again. I will bandage the injured and strengthen the weak. (NLT)

Luke 19:10 "For the Son of Man came to seek and save those who are lost." (NLT)

LET'S APPLY IT!

1. Salvation: Turn back to God and let Him give you a new heart! *Ezekiel 36:26-27*

2. Let God resurrect your spiritual life by:

   - Running to His word daily. *"...dry bones hear the Word of the Lord..."*

   - Every day, invite the Holy Spirit to breathe on your life.

DANIEL

Book: 27 of 66

Author: Daniel is the writer. He is named specifically in Daniel 9:2 & 10:2. Daniel was a young Jewish prince carried off with his friends (Shadrach, Meshach, and Abednego) into captivity to Babylon in 605 B.C. He then became an aid to the kings of Babylon & Persia.

Type of Literature: Chapters 1-6 are history and cover the adventures of life in Babylon for Daniel and his three Jewish friends. In these chapters, we have some of the most famous stories in the Bible: Daniel's fast (1), Nebuchadnezzar's dream (2), the fiery furnace (3), Belshazzar's feast (5), and the lion's den (6).

Chapters 7-12 are prophecy and they tell the future regarding the end times. This section parallels the Book of Revelation.

Audience: Daniel wrote to the Jews exiled in Babylon for three reasons:
1. He is giving a written record of his life.
2. To give encouragement to God's people to stand for God.
3. To tell of the future about the end of time.

Date of Writing: Likely written between 540 - 530 B.C.

Time Period Covered: Daniel served under four different Babylonian and Persian kings: Nebuchadnezzar, Belshazzar, Darius, and lastly Cyrus. (605 B.C - 530 B.C.)

BIG IDEA OF DANIEL:
Believers must stand strong for God in a corrupt culture.

Daniel and his friends stand for God in 3 simple ways:

1. Daniel refuses to conform to the culture and its temptations.

Daniel 1:8 But Daniel was <u>determined not to defile himself</u> by eating the food and wine given to them by the king. He asked the chief of staff for permission not to eat these unacceptable foods. (NLT)

Exodus 23:2 "You must not follow the crowd in doing wrong..." (NLT)

Romans 12:2 ...<u>do not be conformed to this world</u>, but be transformed by the renewing of your mind, that you may prove what is that good and acceptable and perfect will of God.

2. Daniel's three friends refuse to worship a false god made of gold.

Daniel 3:15-18 "I will give you one more chance to bow down and worship the statue I have made when you hear the sound of the musical instruments. But if you refuse, you will be thrown immediately into the blazing furnace. And then what god will be able to rescue you from my power?" Shadrach, Meshach, and Abednego replied, "O Nebuchadnezzar, we do not need to defend ourselves before you. If we are thrown into the blazing furnace, the God whom we serve is able to save us. He will rescue us from your power, Your Majesty. <u>But even if he doesn't</u>, we want to make it clear to you, Your Majesty, that <u>we will never serve your gods or worship the GOLD statue you have set up</u>." (NLT)

I Timothy 6:9 ...those who desire to be rich fall into temptation and a snare, and into many foolish and harmful lusts which drown men in destruction and perdition.

Matthew 6:24 "No one can serve two masters. For you will hate one and love the other; you will be devoted to one and despise the other. You cannot serve God and be enslaved to money." (NLT)

3. Daniel refuses to be quiet about his faith, even when threatened with death.

Daniel 6:7b-10 "Give orders that for the next thirty days any person who prays to anyone, divine or human—except to you, Your Majesty—will be thrown into the den of lions. And now, Your Majesty, issue and sign this law so it cannot be changed" ...So King Darius signed the law. But when Daniel learned that the law had been signed, he went home and knelt down as usual in his upstairs room, <u>with its windows open toward Jerusalem</u>. *He prayed three times a day, just as he had always done, giving thanks to his God. (NLT)*

Romans 1:16 For I am not ashamed of the gospel of Christ, for it is the power of God to salvation for everyone who believes, for the Jew first and also for the Greek.

✝ JESUS IN DANIEL

- **When we stand for Jesus, He stands with us!**

  Daniel 3:25 "Look!" he answered, "I see four men loose, walking in the midst of the fire; and they are not hurt, and the form of the fourth is like the Son of God."

LET'S APPLY IT!

1. Don't conform to corrupt culture; only conform to Christ!

2. Don't bow to gold false gods. Instead, make your gold bow to Jesus.

3. Stand for Jesus and He will stand with you!

   Matthew 10:32 "Everyone who acknowledges me publicly here on earth, I will also acknowledge before my Father in heaven." (NLT)

HOSEA

📠 **Book:** 28 of 66

👤 **Author:** Hosea 1:1 identifies the prophet Hosea as the author. He is known as the preacher with the "broken heart." His writing shows a tender heart of compassion and concern for the people of Israel.

📝 **Type of Literature:** Hosea is a prophecy/sermon of God's unconditional love for people despite their sin. Dr. James Boice refers to the book of Hosea as the "second greatest story in the Bible" after that of Jesus.

🌐 **Audience:** Hosea wrote his sermon to the northern kingdom of Israel. These people lived in open rebellion to God's Word and were known for demonic idol worship and dysfunctional living.

📅 **Date of Writing:** Hosea wrote near the end of his life in 710 B.C.

🕐 **Time Period Covered:** Hosea prophesied during the reigns of six evil kings of Israel, from 755 BC - 710 B.C.

BIG IDEA OF HOSEA:
God loves us with an unending, relentless love.
Hosea reveals God as lovesick husband who has been
cheated on by his wife and he just wants to win her back.

THE BASICS OF THE STORY:

- God tells Hosea to marry a young woman named Gomer.

- Rather than being faithful, Gomer cheats on him repeatedly and lives as a prostitute.

- God tells Hosea to love her and be good to her anyway.

- Gomer has three children by three different men and God tells Hosea to love her relentlessly anyway.

🔑 Key Verses:

1. **God tells Israel - I LOVE YOU!**

   Hosea 2:19-20 "I will make you my wife forever, showing you righteousness and justice, unfailing love and compassion. I will be faithful to you and make you mine, and you will finally know me as the Lord." (NLT)

2. **God tells Israel - You broke my heart and cheated on me with multiple lovers.**

   Hosea 1:2 "Go and marry a prostitute, so that some of her children will be conceived in prostitution. This will illustrate how Israel has acted like a prostitute by turning against the LORD and worshiping other gods."

3. **God tells Israel - I will run after you and seek to win you back.**

   Hosea 2:13-14 "...she put on her earrings and jewels and went out to look for her lovers but forgot all about me," says the LORD. "But then I will win her back once again. I will lead her into the desert and speak tenderly to her there." (NLT)

4. **God tells Israel - I LOVE YOU anyway! Come back to Me!**

   Hosea 3:1 Then the LORD said to me, "Go and love your wife again, even though she commits adultery with another lover. This will illustrate that the LORD still loves Israel, even though the people have turned to other gods and love to worship them." (NLT)

   Hosea 14:1-2, 4 Return, O Israel, to the Lord your God, for your sins have brought you down. Bring your confessions, and return to the Lord. Say to him, "Forgive all our sins and graciously receive us, so that we may offer you our praises. The Lord says, "Then I will heal you of your faithlessness; my love will know no bounds, for my anger will be gone forever." (NLT)

✝ JESUS IN HOSEA

- **Jesus' death, our healing, and resurrection predicted.**

  Hosea 6:1-2 Come, and let us return to the LORD; For He has torn, but He will heal us; He has stricken, but He will bind us up. After two days He will revive us; On the third day He will raise us up, That we may live in His sight.

LET'S APPLY IT!

- The BIG Question:

  ARE YOU CHEATING ON CHRIST? What are the idols in your life that cause you to "cheat on Christ"?

  Hosea 14:8 "O Israel, stay away from idols! I am the one who answers your prayers and cares for you..." (NLT)

- What is an idol?

  Anything you love more than Jesus is an idol. Anything you are devoted to with time and money can be an idol.

- How God expects us to deal with idols:

  Joshua 24:23 "All right then," Joshua said, "destroy the idols among you, and turn your hearts to the LORD, the God of Israel." (NLT)

Books: 29, 30 & 31 of 66

Authors: The titles tell us the writer of each of these books. Joel wrote Joel, Amos wrote Amos, and Obadiah wrote Obadiah.

Type of Literature: These books are prophecy/sermons written to the people of God.

Date of Writing: Joel was written around 835 B.C., Amos around 760 B.C., and Obadiah around 570 B.C.

BIG IDEA OF JOEL:
The "Day of the Lord" is coming soon!

Joel 2:28-29 "Then, after doing all those things, I will pour out my Spirit upon all people. Your sons and daughters will prophesy. Your old men will dream dreams, and your young men will see visions. In those days I will pour out my Spirit even on servants—men and women alike." (NLT)

- This is a reference to Acts 2 and the Holy Spirit falling on us.

Joel 2:30-31 "And I will cause wonders in the heavens and on the earth— blood and fire and columns of smoke. The sun will become dark, and the moon will turn blood red before that great and terrible day of the LORD arrives." (NLT)

- This is a reference to what it will be like in the final days - lots of global upheaval.

JESUS IN JOEL

Joel 2:32 "…everyone who calls on the name of the Lord will be saved." (NLT)

Acts 4:12 "…for there is no other name under heaven given among men by which we must be saved."

BIG IDEA OF AMOS:
In the end, God will judge the nations that oppose Israel.

- Syria - 1:3-5
- Gaza (Philistines) - 1:6-8
- Tyre - 1:9-10
- Edom - 1:11-12
- Ammon - 1:13-15
- Moab - 2:1-3

Genesis 12:3 "I will bless those who bless you and <u>curse those who curse you</u>." (BSB)

✝ JESUS IN AMOS

Amos 9:11-12 "<u>In that day I will restore the fallen house of David</u> [Jesus]. I will repair its damaged walls. From the ruins I will rebuild it and restore its former glory. And Israel will possess what is left of Edom and all the <u>nations I have called to be mine</u> [that's us!]." The LORD has spoken, and he will do these things. (NLT)

BIG IDEA OF OBADIAH:
The "Day of the Lord" is coming for Israel's enemies & everyone.

Obadiah 1:15 "For the day of the LORD upon all the nations is near; <u>As you have done, it shall be done to you</u>; Your reprisal shall return upon your own head."

Revelation 20:11-15 Then I saw a great white throne and Him who sat on it, from whose face the earth and the heaven fled away. And there was found no place for them. And I saw the dead, small and great, standing before God, and books were opened. And another book was opened, which is the Book of Life. <u>And the dead were judged according to their works</u>, by the things which were written in the books. The sea gave up the dead who were in it, and Death and Hades delivered up the dead who were in them. And they were judged, <u>each one according to his works</u>. Then Death and Hades were cast into the lake of fire. This is the second death. And anyone not found written in the Book of Life was cast into the lake of fire.

✝ JESUS IN OBADIAH

Obadiah 1:21 Then <u>saviors</u> shall come to Mount Zion To judge the mountains of Esau, And the <u>kingdom shall be the LORD's</u>.

Revelation 20:6 ...but they shall be priests of God and of Christ, and shall reign with Him a thousand years.

LET'S APPLY IT!

1. **Be ready! The Day of the Lord is near! Jesus is coming soon!**

   Luke 21:25-28 "And there will be signs in the sun, in the moon, and in the stars; and on the earth distress of nations, with perplexity, the sea and the waves roaring; men's hearts failing them from fear and the expectation of those things which are coming on the earth, for the powers of the heavens will be shaken. Then they will see the Son of Man coming in a cloud with power and great glory. Now when these things begin to happen, look up and lift up your heads, because your redemption draws near."

2. **Be rescuing! Help as many people as you can cross the line of faith and follow Jesus before He returns!**

   Jude 1:23 Rescue others by snatching them from the flames of judgment... (NLT)

JONAH

📖 **Book:** 32 of 66

🎯 **Author:** Most theologians point to Jonah the grumpy prophet as the author. He is grumpy because he does not want to go to Nineveh and preach (Jonah 1), and he is unhappy when the city repents and God spares them (Jonah 3-4).

📝 **Type of Literature:** Narrative/History. This story is Jonah's testimony of God working in his life and in the lives of the people of Nineveh.

📅 **Date of Writing:** Likely written between 793 and 758 B.C.

BIG IDEA OF JONAH:
God loves the Gentiles, too! Even the people of God's enemies deserve a chance to repent.

2 Peter 3:9 [God] does not want anyone to be destroyed, but wants everyone to repent. (NLT)

A summary of the book:

- God says go to Nineveh & preach. (1:1-2)

- Jonah rebels and buys a ticket to get on a ship that's going in the opposite direction toward Tarshish, Spain. (1:3)

- God sends a massive storm to stop Jonah. (1:4-9)

- Jonah says the only way to save their lives is to throw him overboard. (1:10-14)

- The sailors throw Jonah over and the storm instantly stops. (1:15-16)

- God has Jonah swallowed by a giant fish. (1:17)

- Jonah is trapped inside the fish for 3 days. (1:17)

- Eventually Jonah repents. (2:1-9)

- God has the fish throw up Jonah on the shore. (2:10)

- God tells Jonah to go to Nineveh again. This time he obeys. (3:1-3)

- Nineveh is so large it takes 3 full days to walk around the city. (3:3) There are at least 120,000 kids in the city. (4:11)

- The city repents and turns back to God, and God spares the city. (3:6-10)

🔑 Key Verse:

*Jonah 1:1-2 The L*ORD *gave this message to Jonah son of Amittai: "Get up and go to the great city of Nineveh. Announce my judgment against it…" (NLT)*

Matthew 28:19 …"GO and make disciples of all the nations, baptizing them in the name of the Father and the Son and the Holy Spirit." (NLT)

Mark 16:15 …He told them, "GO into all the world and preach the GOOD NEWS to everyone." (NLT)

Luke 14:23 Then the master told his servant, "GO out to the roads and country lanes and compel them to come in, so that my house will be full." (NIV)

John 20:21 …"As the Father has sent me, so I am sending you." (NLT)

✝ JESUS IN JONAH

- **Like Jonah was in the belly of a fish for three days and returns, Jesus was in the grave three days and resurrects.**

  Matthew 12:39-41 "…the only sign I will give them is the sign of the prophet Jonah. For as Jonah was in the belly of the great fish for three days and three nights, so will the Son of Man be in the heart of the earth for three days and three nights. The people of Nineveh will stand up against this generation on judgment day and condemn it, for they repented of their sins at the preaching of Jonah. Now someone greater than Jonah is here—but you refuse to repent." (NLT)

LET'S APPLY IT!

1. As a believer, you are Jonah! Don't live in disobedience to God! GO share your faith!

2. Are you living in rebellion like Nineveh? God has so much grace for you if you will repent and turn back to Him!

MICAH, NAHUM & HABBAKUK

📑 **Books:** 33, 34 & 35 of 66

👤 **Authors:** The title of each book tells us who the writers were. Micah wrote Micah, Nahum wrote Nahum, and Habakkuk wrote Habakkuk.

🖊 **Type of Literature:** These books are prophecy/sermons written to the people of God.

📅 **Date of Writing:** Micah wrote between 750-686 B.C. and witnessed the fall of the Northern Kingdom of Israel in 722 B.C. to the Assyrian Empire. Nahum wrote between 663-612 B.C. and Habakkuk wrote between 609-605 B.C., right before the destruction of Jerusalem by the Babylonians in 586 B.C.

BIG IDEA OF MICAH:
God desires real faith, not religion!

Micah 6:8 He has shown you oh man, what is good; And what does the LORD require of you; But to do justly, To love mercy, And to walk humbly with your God?

✝ JESUS IN MICAH

- **Christ's future reign:**

  Micah 4:1-2 Now it shall come to pass in the latter days That the mountain of the LORD's house Shall be established on the top of the mountains, And shall be exalted above the hills; And peoples shall flow to it. Many nations shall come and say, "Come, and let us go up to the mountain of the LORD, To the house of the God of Jacob; He will teach us His ways, And we shall walk in His paths."

- **Christ's birthplace:**

  Micah 5:2 "But you, Bethlehem Ephrathah, Though you are little among the thousands of Judah, Yet out of you shall come forth to Me The One to be Ruler in Israel, Whose goings forth are from of old, From everlasting."

BIG IDEA OF NAHUM:
God's judgment is coming to Nineveh.

Nahum 1:3 The LORD is slow to get angry, but his power is great, and he never lets the guilty go unpunished... (NLT)

✝ JESUS IN NAHUM

Nahum 1:15 "Look! A messenger is coming over the mountains with good news! He is bringing a message of peace..." (NLT)

BIG IDEA OF HABAKKUK:
Trusting God's goodness gets us through our moments of grief.

Habakkuk 1:2-3 How long, O LORD, must I call for help? But you do not listen! "Violence is everywhere!" I cry, but you do not come to save. Must I forever see these evil deeds? Why must I watch all this misery? Wherever I look, I see destruction and violence... (NLT)

Habakkuk 3:17-19 Though the fig tree may not blossom, Nor fruit be on the vines; Though the labor of the olive may fail, And the fields yield no food; Though the flock may be cut off from the fold, And there be no herd in the stalls—Yet I will rejoice in the LORD, I will joy in the God of my salvation. The LORD God is my strength; He will make my feet like deer's feet, And He will make me walk on my high hills.

✝ JESUS IN HABAKKUK:

* **Jesus' name means: "God is salvation."**

    Habakkuk 3:18 ...I will joy in the <u>God of my salvation</u>.

LET'S APPLY IT!

- Micah - Real faith, not religion, transforms. Are we religious or in real relationship with Christ?

- Nahum - Judgment came for Nineveh. Are we ready to meet our Judge?

- Habakkuk - Pain happens to everyone. Will we trust that God is good despite our circumstances?

  Habakkuk 2:4 ...the just shall live by his faith.

  Acts 16:31,33 "Believe on the Lord Jesus Christ, and you will be saved, you and your household..." And immediately he and all his family were baptized.

ZEPHANIAH, HAGGAI & ZECHARIAH

Books: 36, 37 & 38 of 66

Authors: The title of each book tells us who the writers were. Zephaniah was written by Zephaniah. Haggai was written by Haggai. Zechariah was written by Zechariah.

Type of Literature: These books are prophecy/sermons written to the people of God.

2 Peter 1:21 ...for prophecy never came by the will of man, but holy men of God spoke as they were moved by the Holy Spirit.

Date of Writing: Zephaniah wrote between 635-625 B.C. before Jerusalem was destroyed in 586 B.C. Haggai wrote around 520 B.C. after the Jews returned from Babylon. Zechariah wrote at the same time or soon after Haggai between 520 - 470 B.C.

BIG IDEA OF ZEPHANIAH:
"The Day of the Lord" (End of Days) is coming!
God will bring blessing or judgment. Pick a side.

Blessing for God's people:

Zephaniah 3:9-12 "...I will purify the speech of all people, so that everyone can worship the LORD together... On that day you will no longer need to be ashamed, for you will no longer be rebels against me... Those who are left will be the lowly and humble for it is they who trust in the name of the LORD." (NLT)

Judgment for God's enemies:

Zephaniah 1:18 Neither their silver nor their gold Shall be able to deliver them In the day of the LORD's wrath...

✝ JESUS IN ZEPHANIAH:

Zephaniah 3:17 "The LORD your God in your midst, The Mighty One, will save; He will rejoice over you with gladness, He will quiet you with His love, He will rejoice over you with singing."

BIG IDEA OF HAGGAI:
The Lord's House.
Don't forget to build God's House not just your own!

Haggai 1:4-8 "Is it time for you yourselves to dwell in your paneled houses, and this temple to lie in ruins?" Now therefore, thus says the LORD of hosts: "Consider your ways! You have sown much, and bring in little; You eat, but do not have enough; You drink, but you are not filled with drink; You clothe yourselves, but no one is warm; And he who earns wages, Earns wages to put into a bag with holes." Thus says the LORD of hosts: "Consider your ways! Go up to the mountains and bring wood and build the temple, that I may take pleasure in it and be glorified," says the Lord.

✝ JESUS IN HAGGAI:

Haggai 2:7-9 "I will <u>shake all the nations,</u> and the treasures of all the nations will be brought to this Temple. <u>I will fill this place with glory,</u> says the LORD of Heaven's Armies… <u>The future glory of this Temple will be greater than its past glory,</u> says the LORD of Heaven's Armies. And in this place <u>I will bring peace.</u> I, the LORD of Heaven's Armies, have spoken."

BIG IDEA OF ZECHARIAH:
Restoration. Christ will fix all things!
(Zechariah says more about Jesus' first and second coming than all the other books of the minor prophets.)

Jesus' First Coming:

- He will enter Jerusalem on a colt. (9:9)

- He will be betrayed for 30 pieces of silver. (11:12)

- He will be struck and His followers scattered. (13:7)

- He will be pierced. (12:10)

- He will remove our sin in a single day. (3:9)

Jesus' Second Coming:

- The Jews will return to Jesus. They will "look on the one they have pierced" and mourn for "their firstborn son." (12:10)

- At His return, He will land on the Mount of Olives. (14:4)

- He will defeat His enemies in a giant battle. (14:12-15)

- He will rebuild His temple and rule the world from Jerusalem. (6:12-13; 14:9)

- All the world will come to Jerusalem to worship and serve Him. (14:16)

LET'S APPLY IT!

- Zephaniah - The end is coming! Pick a side!

- Haggai - Christ is coming! Build His house, not just your house!

- Zechariah - Christ will restore all things. What do you need Him to restore?

MALACHI

📖 **Book:** 39 of 66

👤 **Author:** Malachi is named as the writer in 1:1. He is the last prophet of God before the "400 Silent Years". The next prophet of God did not come until John the Baptist when he announces the arrival of Jesus.

Malachi 4:5-6 "Look, I am sending you the prophet Elijah before the great and dreadful day of the Lord arrives. His preaching will turn the hearts of fathers to their children, and the hearts of children to their fathers..." (NLT)

📅 **Date of Writing:** Around 430 B.C., after the Jews have returned from Babylonian captivity.

✍️ **Type of Literature:** Sermon/prophecy. This book is God's last word to the nation of Israel before Jesus arrives.

🌐 **Audience:** The Jews are spiritually numb and going through the motions of worship. (No heart.)

BIG IDEA OF MALACHI:
True worship. Four aspects of real, heartfelt worship.

1. True Worshippers = Bring their best.

Malachi 1:6-8 ..."A son honors his father, and a servant respects his master. If I am your father and master, where are the honor and respect I deserve? You have shown contempt for my name! "But you ask, 'How have we ever shown contempt for your name?' "You have shown contempt by offering defiled sacrifices on my altar. "Then you ask, 'How have we defiled the sacrifices? "You defile them by saying the altar of the Lord deserves no respect. When you give blind animals as sacrifices, isn't that wrong? And isn't it wrong to offer animals that are crippled and diseased? Try giving gifts like that to your governor, and see how pleased he is!"... (NLT)

2. True Worshippers = Love their spouse.

Malachi 2:14-16 You cry out, "Why doesn't the LORD accept my worship?" I'll tell you why! Because the LORD witnessed the vows you and your wife made when you were young. But you have been unfaithful to her, though she remained your faithful partner, the wife of your marriage vows. Didn't the LORD make you one with your wife? In body and spirit you are his. And what does he want? Godly children from your union. So guard your heart; remain loyal to the wife of your youth. "For I hate divorce!" says the LORD, the God of Israel. "To divorce your wife is to overwhelm her with cruelty," says the LORD of Heaven's Armies. "So guard your heart; do not be unfaithful to your wife." (NLT)

3. True Worshippers = Bring the tithe.

Malachi 3:8-12 "Should people cheat God? Yet you have cheated me! "But you ask, 'What do you mean? When did we ever cheat you?' "You have cheated me of the tithes and offerings due to me. You are under a curse, for your whole nation has been cheating me. Bring all the tithes into the storehouse so there will be enough food in my Temple. If you do," says the LORD of Heaven's Armies, "I will open the windows of heaven for you. I will pour out a blessing so great you won't have enough room to take it in! Try it! Put me to the test! Your crops will be abundant, for I will guard them from insects and disease. Your grapes will not fall from the vine before they are ripe," says the LORD of Heaven's Armies. "Then all nations will call you blessed..." (NLT)

4. True Worshippers = Look for Jesus' return.

✝ JESUS IN MALACHI:

Malachi 4:2 "...for you who fear my name, the Sun of Righteousness will rise with healing in his wings. And you will go free, leaping with joy like calves let out to pasture." (NLT)

Matthew 24:42-44 "So you, too, must keep watch! For you don't know what day your Lord is coming. Understand this: If a homeowner knew exactly when a burglar was coming, he would keep watch and not permit his house to be broken into. You also must be ready all the time, for the Son of Man will come when least expected." (NLT)

LET'S APPLY IT!

1. Bring your best to worship.

2. Love your spouse.

3. Bring the tithe.

4. Look for Jesus.

📖 **Book:** 40 of 66

🔘 **Author:** Matthew. Matthew was a tax collector that Jesus calls out of his dysfunctional life to follow Him (Matthew 9:9-13). Matthew becomes one of the original 12 disciples.

✏️ **Type of Literature:** History/story. Matthew is one of four gospels, telling us the "good news" of Jesus.

🌐 **Audience:** Matthew writes to a Jewish audience, seeking to help his people connect with Christ. He starts his book with a genealogy specific to Abraham and David as Jewish leaders. He identifies Jesus as from the tribe of Judah and he quotes from the Old Testament more than sixty times to connect with his Jewish audience.

The reason there are 4 gospels:

Each gospel has a different audience and different focus.

Gospel	Matthew	Mark	Luke	John
Audience	Jewish	Roman	Greeks	Everyone
Focus	Jesus is the "Messiah/King" predicted in the OT.	Jesus is the "suffering servant" who ministers to our needs.	Jesus is the perfect "Son of Man" come to save us.	Jesus is God in the flesh.

📅 **Date of Writing:** Matthew writes after the events of Jesus' life. It is his memories of his time with Jesus. The most likely date of writing is somewhere around 62-69 A.D.

🕐 **Time Period Covered:** The gospel of Matthew is entirely focused on the life of Christ. Jesus is born around 3/4 B.C. and dies and resurrects around 30 A.D.

BIG IDEA OF MATTHEW:
Jesus is the one true king.

10 WAYS MATTHEW MAKES HIS CASE:

1. **Jesus' ancestry proves Jesus is the one true king.**

    *   *Matthew 1* - Genealogy from Abraham to David to Jesus.

2. **Jesus' birth proves He is one true king.**

    *   *Matthew 1:21 "...she will have a son, and you are to name him Jesus, for he will save his people from their sins." (NLT)*

    *   *Matthew 2:2 ..."Where is the One who is BORN KING of the Jews?"... (NIV)*

3. **Jesus' baptism proves He is the one true king.**

    *   *Matthew 3:17 ...suddenly a voice came from heaven, saying, "This is My beloved Son, in whom I am well pleased."*

    *   He is God approved. He is the royalty of heaven.

4. **Jesus' temptation proves He is the one true king.**

    *   *Matthew 4*

    *   The "King of Heaven" defeats the "king of darkness" three times.

5. **Jesus' teaching proves He is the one true king.**

    *   Jesus' main message: *Matthew 4:17 From that time Jesus began to preach and to say, "Repent, for <u>the kingdom of heaven</u> is at hand."*

    *   56 times the word "Kingdom" is used.

    *   32 times the phrase "Kingdom of Heaven" is used.

6. Jesus' miracles prove He is the one true king.

- In Matthew 8-9, Jesus does ten miracles.

- *Isaiah 35:5-6 ...when he comes, he will open the eyes of the blind and unplug the ears of the deaf. The lame will leap like a deer, and those who cannot speak will sing for joy... (NLT)*

7. Jesus' triumphal entry proves He is the one true king.
(Matthew 21)

- *Zechariah 9:9 ...Look, your king is coming to you. He is righteous and victorious, yet he is humble, riding on a donkey... (NLT)*

- He is King of kings over all human governments.

8. Jesus' death & blood prove He is the one true king.

- *Matthew 26:28 ...this is My blood of the new covenant, which is shed for many for the remission of sins.*

- His royal blood conquers our sin.

9. Jesus' resurrection proves He is the one true king.

- *Matthew 28:6 "He isn't here! He is risen from the dead, just as He said would happen..."*

- He is king over death.

10. Jesus' final words prove He is the one true king.

- *Matthew 28:18-19 Jesus came and spoke to them, saying, "All AUTHORITY has been given to Me in heaven and on earth. Go therefore and make disciples of all the nations, baptizing them in the name of the Father and of the Son and of the Holy Spirit..."*

LET'S APPLY IT!

1. If Jesus is the one true king - who sits on the throne of your life?

    Matthew 10:32-33 "Everyone who acknowledges me publicly here on earth, I will also acknowledge before my Father in heaven. But everyone who denies me here on earth, I will also deny before my Father in heaven." (NLT)

2. If Jesus is your one true king - will you seek His Kingdom above your own?

    Matthew 6:33 "...Seek <u>FIRST HIS KINGDOM</u> and His righteousness and all these things will be added unto you." (BSB)

    Matthew 6:10 "<u>YOUR KINGDOM COME</u>, Your will be done On earth as it is in heaven."

3. If Jesus is your one true king - will you proclaim His kingdom to others?

    Matthew 28:19 "<u>Go therefore and make disciples</u> of all the nations, baptizing them in the name of the Father and of the Son and of the Holy Spirit..."

Book: 41 of 66

Author: John Mark.

- He was a cousin of Barnabas and traveled with Paul on Paul's first missionary journey.
- Mark got discouraged and quit, irritating Paul who refused to take Mark on his second missionary trip.
- Paul & Mark later reconciled (Colossians 4:10; Philemon 1:24).
- Eventually he served with the Apostle Peter in Rome. During this time, Peter shared his memories of Jesus and Mark wrote them down. Therefore, one could call this gospel the "Gospel of Peter".
- Mark became a church planter in North Africa and started the Alexandria, Egypt church where he was eventually martyred.

Type of Literature: History/story. Mark is one of four gospels telling us the "good news" of Jesus.

Audience: Mark is not Jewish, so he writes to a non-Jewish Roman audience. Romans were "get things done" type people so the book is action-oriented and focused on what Jesus did and less on what He said (Matthew gives us 14 parables, Mark gives us 4). Mark is the shortest gospel and almost reads like bullet points on the life of Christ.

Date of Writing: Mark writes down Peter's memories in the early 60's A.D. when Peter and Mark served together in Rome.

Time Period Covered: The Gospel of Mark is focused on the three-year ministry of Christ. Jesus began public ministry around 27 A.D. and dies and resurrects around 30 A.D.

BIG IDEA OF MARK:
Jesus is the suffering servant of God.

Mark 10:45 "...the Son of Man did not come to be served, but to serve, and to give His life a ransom for many."

MARK BREAKS HIS GOSPEL UP INTO 3 PARTS

Part 1 - Jesus came to serve us (Mark 1-8).
(Jesus serves us by casting out demons, healing the sick, feeding thousands, calming storms, and raising the dead.)

One example:

Mark 5:35-36;40-42 While He was still speaking, some came from the ruler of the synagogue's house who said, "Your daughter is dead. Why trouble the Teacher any further?" As soon as Jesus heard the word that was spoken, He said to the ruler of the synagogue, "Do not be afraid; only believe." ...He took the father and the mother of the child, and those who were with Him, and entered where the child was lying. Then He took the child by the hand, and said to her, "Talitha, cumi," which is translated, "Little girl, I say to you, arise." Immediately the girl arose and walked, for she was twelve years of age. And they were overcome with great amazement.

Part 2 - Jesus came to suffer for us (Mark 9-15).
(Jesus suffers in prayer in the garden, through betrayal and false trial, through beating and mockery, torture and crucifixion.)

One example:

Mark 15:15-20; 22-24 So Pilate... delivered Jesus, after he had <u>scourged</u> Him, to be crucified. Then the soldiers led Him away into the hall called Praetorium, and they called together the whole garrison. And they clothed Him with purple; and they twisted a <u>crown of thorns</u>, put it on His head, and began to salute Him, "Hail, King of the Jews!" Then they struck Him on the head with a reed and spat on Him; and bowing the knee, they worshiped Him. And when they had mocked Him, they <u>took the purple off</u> Him, put His own clothes on Him, and led Him out to crucify Him. And they brought Him to the place <u>Golgotha</u>, which is translated, <u>Place of a Skull</u>... And when they <u>crucified</u> Him...

Part 3 - Jesus the suffering servant conquered death for us!

Mark 16:6-7 But [the angel] said to them, "Do not be alarmed. You seek Jesus of Nazareth, who was crucified. <u>He is risen</u>! He is not here. See the place where they laid Him. But go, tell His disciples—and Peter—that He is going before you into Galilee; there you will see Him, as <u>He said to you</u>."

I Corinthians 15:57 But thank God! He gives us victory over sin and death through our Lord Jesus Christ. (NLT)

LET'S APPLY IT!

1. Will you follow the One who conquered sin and death for you?

   Mark 16:16 "He who believes and is baptized will be saved; but he who does not believe will be condemned."

2. Will you serve others like Jesus served?

   Mark 10:44 "…whoever wants to be first among you must be the slave [servant] of everyone else." (NLT)

3. Will you tell the world of the suffering servant who died and rose for them?

   Mark 16:14-16 Later He appeared to the eleven as they sat at the table; and He rebuked their unbelief and hardness of heart, because they did not believe those who had seen Him after He had risen. And He said to them, "<u>Go into all the world and preach the gospel to every creature</u>. He who believes and is baptized will be saved; but he who does not believe will be condemned."

LUKE

👤 **Author:** Luke. He was a Gentile doctor who researched the life of Jesus and interviewed the eyewitnesses to Jesus' life. He then wrote the longest, most detailed account on the life of Christ.

✏️ **Type of Literature:** History/story. Luke is one of four gospels telling us the "good news" of Jesus.

🌐 **Audience:** Luke writes to a Greek friend named Theophilus (1:3). Therefore, his writing would have appealed to the Greeks as a whole. The Greeks were the "influencers" of the Roman Empire. Culture, religion, education, and language all had their foundation in Greek ideology. So this book would have gained wide traction across the entire Roman Empire.

📅 **Date of Writing:** Since Luke is interviewing eyewitnesses to Jesus' life, his research would probably have happened between A.D. 40-60, putting his completed book around A.D. 60–65.

🕐 **Time Period Covered:** The Gospel of Luke is focused on the entire life of Christ. Jesus is born around 3/4 B.C. and dies and resurrects around 30 A.D.

BIG IDEA OF LUKE:
Jesus is the perfect "Son of Man".

- God became 100% human.

- This human (Jesus) was the only perfect human.

- This human (Jesus) died in our place for our sins, because He is one of us.

🔑 Key verse:
Luke 19:10 "... the Son of Man has come to seek and to save that which was lost."

This verse is the outline of the entire Book of Luke:

1. **"... the Son of Man has come..."** - **Jesus came from Heaven to Earth to be like us.** (Chapters 1-3)

   Luke 1:30-32 Then the angel said to her, "Do not be afraid, Mary, for you have found favor with God. And behold, you will conceive in your womb and <u>bring forth a Son,</u> [100% human] and shall call His name JESUS. He will be great, and will be called the Son of the Highest..." (100% God, from Heaven in flesh.)

   Hebrews 4:15 For we do not have a High Priest [Jesus] who cannot sympathize with our weaknesses, but was in all points tempted as we are, yet without sin.

2. **"...to seek..."** - **Jesus came to seek us out. He was on an all-out search to find us and bring us back into relationship with Himself.** (Chapters 4-19)

   Luke 4:18-19 "The Spirit of the LORD is upon me, for he has anointed me to bring Good News to the poor. He has sent me to proclaim that captives will be released, that the blind will see that the oppressed will be set free, and that the time of the LORD's favor has come." (NLT)

   Luke 15:3-7 So Jesus told them this story: "If a man has a hundred sheep and one of them gets lost, what will he do? <u>Won't he leave the ninety-nine others in the wilderness and go to search for the one that is lost until he finds it?</u> And when he has found it, he will joyfully carry it home on his shoulders. When he arrives, he will call together his friends and neighbors, saying, 'Rejoice with me because I have found my lost sheep.' <u>In the same way, there is more joy in heaven over one lost sinner who repents and returns to God</u> than over ninety-nine others who are righteous and haven't strayed away!" (NLT)

3. **"...and to SAVE that which was lost." - Jesus came to rescue us from our sin and dysfunction through the cross and resurrection.** (Chapters 20-24)

Luke 23:33-34 When they came to a place called The Skull, they nailed him to the cross. And the criminals were also crucified—one on his right and one on his left. Jesus said, "<u>Father, forgive them</u>, for they don't know what they are doing..." (NLT)

Luke 24:38-41, 44-48 "Why are you frightened?" he asked. "<u>Why are your hearts filled with doubt? Look at my hands. Look at my feet. You can see that it's really me</u>. Touch me and make sure that I am not a ghost, because ghosts don't have bodies, as you see that I do." As he spoke, he showed them his hands and his feet. Still they stood there in disbelief, filled with joy and wonder... Then he said, "When I was with you before, I told you that everything written about me in the law of Moses and the prophets and in the Psalms must be fulfilled." Then he opened their minds to understand the Scriptures. And he said, "Yes, it was written long ago <u>that the Messiah would suffer and die and rise from the dead on the third day</u>. It was also written that this message would be proclaimed in the authority of his name to all the nations, beginning in Jerusalem: '<u>There is forgiveness of sins for all who repent</u>.' You are witnesses of all these things." (NLT)

LET'S APPLY IT!

1. Luke writes to tell the world, "Jesus came to seek and save the lost." Are you lost? Come back to God and let Jesus forgive you and free you! *Romans 10:13; Acts 16:31-33*

2. If Luke writes to tell us of the One who "came to seek and save the lost," will you seek and save the lost?

   Luke 14:23 "...Go out into the country lanes and behind the hedges and urge anyone you find to come, so that the house will be full."

Book: 43 of 66

Author: John. The youngest disciple of Jesus. John calls himself "the disciple whom Jesus loved." (I'm his favorite.) (John 13:21-30; 18:15-18; 19:26-27; 21:7; 21:20). We can trust his account to be true because he was boiled in oil (and survived) refusing to recant his story.

Type of Literature: History/story. John is one of four gospels telling us the "good news" of Jesus.

Audience: John writes to a general audience. His gospel is a story, but it is written almost like a sermon. He is preaching to anyone and everyone that Jesus is God!

Date of Writing: Written around 90 A.D., 60 years after the crucifixion. John is an old man and doesn't want the story of Jesus to be forgotten, so he writes down his memories of his time with Jesus. Our oldest copy of John is from 120 A.D.

Time Period Covered: The Gospel of John is focused on the life of Christ. Jesus is born around 3/4 B.C. and dies and resurrects around 30 A.D.

BIG IDEA OF JOHN:
Jesus is God, so believe on Him!

1. **John uses 7 titles to explain Jesus is better than all other gods in Chapter 1:**

   - The Word *(John 1:1, 14)* - Creator of all

   - The Light *(John 1:4-13)* - Light for all people

   - The Son of God *(John 1:14-28, 34, 49)* - Equal with God

   - The Lamb of God *(John 1:29-36)* - Only sacrifice for our sins

   - The Messiah *(John 1:35-42)* - Promised Rescuer

   - The King of Israel *(John 1:43-49)* - Greatest King

   - The Son of Man *(John 1:50-51)* - Perfect human

2. **John describes 7 "signs" proving Jesus is a better God:**

- Turning water into wine *(John 2:1-11)* - God of blessing

- Healing an official's son *(John 4:46-54)* - God of healing

- Healing a lame man at the Pool of Bethesda *(John 5:1-15)* - God of healing

- Healing a man born blind *(John 9:1-7)* - God of healing (Three times = perfection)

- Feeding 5,000 at the Sea of Galilee *(John 6:1-15)* - God of Provision

- Walking on water *(John 6:16-21)* - God over nature

- Raising Lazarus from the dead *(John 11:1-45)* - God of life

  John 11:25 Jesus told her, "I am the resurrection and the LIFE. Anyone who believes in me will live, even after dying." (NLT)

3. **John lists 7 times other people proclaim Him as - "from God or God Himself":**

- John the Baptist *(John 1:29)* - Lamb of God.

- Nathanael *(John 1:49)* - Son of God, King of Israel.

- Peter *(John 6:69)* - Holy One of God.

- The man born blind *(John 9:35-38)* - Declared "Lord" and accepts worship.

- Martha *(John 11:27)* - Messiah, Son of God.

- Thomas - *John 20:28 "My LORD and my GOD."*

- Jesus Himself -

  John 8:58 Jesus answered, "I tell you the truth, before Abraham was even born, I AM! [YHWH]" (NLT)

4. **John shares 7 illustrations Jesus uses to describe Himself as the ONLY one who can save us:**

- I am the Bread of Life *(John 6:35)* - He is our spiritual food.
- I am the Light of the World *(John 8:12)* - He is illumination for our path.
- I am the Door for the Sheep *(John 10:7-9)* - He is the only doorway to Heaven.
- I am the Good Shepherd *(John 10:11)* - He is the Shepherd of our souls.
- I am the Resurrection and the Life *(John 11:25)* - He is life.
- I am the Way, the Truth, and the Life *(John 14:6)*.
- I am the True Vine *(John 15:1)* - He is "The Source" for all things.

5. **John ends his book with these words:**

John 20:31 ...these are written that you may <u>believe</u> that Jesus is the Christ, the Son of God, and that believing you may have <u>LIFE in His name</u>.

LET'S APPLY IT!

1. Jesus is not just a good teacher or a wise man. He is BETTER than all other gods. Is He YOUR God?

   John 14:6 Jesus said, "...I am the WAY, the TRUTH and THE LIFE, no one comes to the Father except through me." (ESV)

   John 3:18 "He who believes in [Jesus] is not condemned; but he who does not believe is condemned already, because he has not believed in the name of the only begotten Son of God."

2. John wrote so you would believe. Will you tell others so they will believe?

   John 20:21 "...As the Father has sent Me, I also SEND YOU."

ACTS

Book: 44 of 66

Author: Luke. Acts is part 2 of the Book of Luke. Luke was a Gentile doctor who traveled with the Apostle Paul. (Colossians 4:14; 2 Timothy 4:11; Philemon 1:24)

Type of Literature: History/story. Acts is a record of the first Christians after the resurrection of Jesus.

Audience: Luke is the only Gentile (non-Jewish) author of the New Testament emphasizing God's plan for all people.

Date of Writing: Acts is likely written between 62-65 A.D. before the Apostle Paul's death, since it is not mentioned in the book.

Time Period Covered: Acts picks up where the Gospel of Luke ends, starting with the ascension of Jesus and the commissioning of the disciples (1:8), and continuing to the end of Paul's first Roman imprisonment in approximately 62 A.D.

BIG IDEA OF ACTS:
The Acts of the Holy Spirit.

Focus:
- The Old Testament - God the Father
- The Gospels - Jesus
- Acts - Holy Spirit

4 things Luke says about the Holy Spirit in the Book of Acts:

1. The Holy Spirit empowers us.

Acts 1:8 "But you shall receive POWER when the Holy Spirit has come upon you; and you shall be witnesses to Me in Jerusalem, and in all Judea and Samaria, and to the end of the earth."

Key word in Greek = *dunamis* (dynamite) = explosive, supernatural power to live and change.

Galatians 5:22-23 But the [supernatural explosive] fruit of the Spirit is love, joy, peace, longsuffering, kindness, goodness, faithfulness, gentleness, self-control...

2. The Holy Spirit fills us.

Acts 2:1-4 On the day of Pentecost all the believers were meeting together in one place. Suddenly, there was a sound from heaven like the roaring of a mighty windstorm, and it filled the house where they were sitting. Then, what looked like flames or tongues of fire appeared and settled on each of them. And <u>everyone present was FILLED with the Holy Spirit</u> and began speaking in other languages... (NLT)

Ephesians 5:18 Don't be drunk with wine, because that will ruin your life. Instead, <u>be filled with the Holy Spirit</u>... (NLT)

Galatians 5:16 ...<u>as you yield</u> to the dynamic life and power of the Holy Spirit, you will abandon the cravings of your self-life. (TPT)

3. He refreshes us.

Acts 3:19-20 ...repent of your sins and turn to God, so that your sins may be wiped away. <u>Then times of refreshment</u> will come from the presence of the Lord... (NLT)

Isaiah 44:3 ...I will pour water on him who is thirsty, And floods on the dry ground; <u>I will pour My Spirit</u> on your descendants...

Ephesians 6:18 Pray in the Spirit at all times and on every occasion... (NLT)

4. The Holy Spirit is a gift. (Received through repentance and faith in Christ.)

Acts 2:38 Then Peter said to them, "<u>Repent,</u> and let every one of you be baptized in the <u>name of Jesus Christ</u> for the remission of sins; and <u>you shall receive the gift of the Holy Spirit.</u>"

LET'S APPLY IT!

1. Will you repent of your sins and be baptized in the name of Jesus?

2. Are you feeling spiritually dry and parched? Your spiritual life will be as refreshed as you stay refilled.

Book: 45 of 66

Author: The Apostle Paul. His Jewish/Hebrew name was Saul, but he changed it to the Greek name Paul after he became a Jesus-follower.

Type of Literature: Epistle. Romans is a letter from Paul.

A Crash Course on Paul:
- Paul was a Jewish Pharisee who hated Christianity and persecuted and killed Christians.
- On a journey to persecute Christians in Damascus, he was confronted on the road by Jesus Himself (Acts 9). This was Christ after His resurrection.
- Paul repented and Jesus forgave and transformed him.
- Eventually Jesus sent Paul to share the gospel with the Gentiles.
- Paul spent the rest of his life traveling the Roman Empire starting churches in pagan cities and preaching about Jesus.
- Paul became the greatest missionary of all time and many of his letters make up much of the New Testament.
- Paul was eventually beheaded by the Emperor Nero in Rome around 67 A.D.

Audience: Romans was written to the Christians living in Rome. Rome was the most powerful city on earth at the time with a population around 1 million people. The few believers in the city met in house churches or in secret at night in the catacombs under the city. They suffered severe persecution from the emperors of Rome for 300 years and had to courageously follow Jesus in a pagan, violent culture where Christianity was illegal.

Date of Writing: 56-58 A.D. (25-30 years after the resurrection of Christ.)

BIG IDEA OF ROMANS:
The Power of the Gospel (Good News).

🔑 **Key verse:**
Romans 1:16 For I am not ashamed of the GOSPEL of Christ, for it is the POWER of God to salvation for everyone who believes...

Chapter 1-3:23: We are powerless. We can't fix ourselves.

Romans 3:10-12, 23 ...No one is righteous—not even one. No one is truly wise; no one is seeking God. All have turned away...No one does good, not a single one. ...For everyone has sinned; we all fall short of God's glorious standard. (NLT)

Chapters 3:24-7:25: The Gospel is powerful. Christ can do what we can never do for ourselves.

Romans 3:23-25 ...for all have sinned and fall short of the glory of God, and all are <u>justified</u> freely by his grace through the redemption that came by Christ Jesus. God presented Christ as a sacrifice of atonement, through the shedding of his blood—to be received by faith... (NIV)

> KEY WORD: Justified (Greek = *dik-ah-yo'-o*) = to make righteous. Just as if I never sinned.

Romans 5:6-9 When we were <u>utterly helpless, Christ came at just the right time and died for us sinners</u>. Now, most people would not be willing to die for an upright person, though someone might perhaps be willing to die for a person who is especially good. But God showed his great love for us by sending Christ to die for us while we were still sinners. And since <u>we have been MADE RIGHT in God's sight by the blood of Christ</u>, he will certainly save us from God's condemnation. (NLT)

Chapters 8:1-11:36: The Gospel's power comes from love.

Romans 8:35-39 Can anything ever separate us from Christ's love? Does it mean he no longer loves us if we have trouble or calamity, or are persecuted, or hungry, or destitute, or in danger, or threatened with death? No, despite all these things, overwhelming victory is ours through Christ, who loved us. And I am convinced that nothing can ever separate us from God's love. Neither death nor life, neither angels nor demons, neither our fears for today nor our worries about tomorrow—not even the powers of hell can separate us from God's love. No power in the sky above or in the earth below—indeed, nothing in all creation will ever be able to separate us from the love of God that is revealed in Christ Jesus our Lord. (NLT)

Chapters 12:1-16:27: The Gospel produces powerful transformation.

Romans 12:2 Don't copy the behavior and customs of this world, but <u>let God transform you into a new person</u> by changing the way you think. Then you will learn to know God's will for you, which is good and pleasing and perfect. (NLT)

Romans 13:11-14 ...time is running out. Wake up, for our salvation is nearer now than when we first believed. The night is almost gone; the day of salvation will soon be here. So <u>remove your dark deeds like dirty clothes</u>, and put on the shining armor of right living. Because we belong to the day, we must live decent lives for all to see. Don't participate in the darkness of wild parties and drunkenness, or in sexual promiscuity and immoral living, or in quarreling and jealousy. <u>Instead, clothe yourself with the presence of the Lord Jesus Christ</u>. And don't let yourself think about ways to indulge your evil desires. (NLT)

LET'S APPLY IT!

1. Will you admit you are powerless and stop trying to fix yourself?

2. Will you receive Christ as Lord? He is the only higher power who can save!

   Romans 10:9-11 If you openly declare that Jesus is Lord and believe in your heart that God raised him from the dead, you will be saved. For it is by believing in your heart that you are made right with God, and it is by openly declaring your faith that you are saved. As the Scriptures tell us, "Anyone who trusts in him will never be disgraced." (NLT)

3. Will you embrace a new way of living powered by the Gospel rather than your own strength?

Book: 46 of 66

Author: The Apostle Paul. His Jewish/Hebrew name was Saul (means "effeminate walk" in Greek). When he became a missionary to the Greeks/Romans, he changed his name to the Latin name Paul (means "humble or least"). He calls himself the "least of the Apostles" (I Cor 15:9).

Type of Literature: Epistle. I Corinthians is a letter from Paul written to the Christians in the Greek city of Corinth.

Audience: This letter was written to the Christians living in Corinth. The city was the center of the Roman Empire for gambling, drunkenness, and prostitution. Sailors and soldiers from all over the Roman Empire would come here for vacation. When they got off the ships, they were greeted by 1,000 male and female prostitutes who worked at the temple Aphrodite.

Setting: According to Acts 18, Paul left the city of Athens and traveled 52 miles east to Corinth. He then started a small church and spent a year teaching the new believers there before moving on.

Date of Writing: Paul writes this letter from the city of Ephesus to the Corinthian believers sometime between 52-55 A.D.

BIG IDEA OF 1 CORINTHIANS:
There is major dysfunction in the Church!

Problem 1 = Divisiveness and conflict.

I Corinthians 1:10-11 I appeal to you, dear brothers and sisters, by the authority of our Lord Jesus Christ, to live in harmony with each other. Let there be no divisions in the church. Rather, be of one mind, united in thought and purpose. For some members of Chloe's household have told me about your quarrels, my dear brothers and sisters. (NLT)

Paul's solution = Church is a team sport. Stop fighting and get along!

I Corinthians 3:1-3 Dear brothers and sisters, when I was with you I couldn't talk to you as I would to spiritual people. I had to talk as though you belonged to this world or as though you were infants in Christ. I had to feed you with milk, not with solid food, because you weren't ready for anything stronger. And you still aren't ready, for you are still controlled by your sinful nature. You are jealous of one another and quarrel with each other. Doesn't that prove you are controlled by your sinful nature? Aren't you living like people of the world? (NLT)

I Corinthians 12:12-13, 25 The human body has many parts, but the many parts make up one whole body. So it is with the body of Christ. Some of us are Jews, some are Gentiles, some are slaves, and some are free. But we have all been baptized into one body by one Spirit, and we all share the same Spirit (NLT) ...that there should be no schism in the body, but that the members should have the same care for one another. (NKJV)

Problem 2 = Sexual misconduct.

I Corinthians 6:13 You say, "Food was made for the stomach, and the stomach for food." (This is true, though someday God will do away with both of them.) But you can't say that our bodies were made for sexual immorality... (NLT)

Paul's solution = Remember your body is the temple of the Holy Spirit! Treat your body that way!

I Corinthians 6:18-20 Run from sexual sin! No other sin so clearly affects the body as this one does. For sexual immorality is a sin against your own body. Don't you realize that your body is the temple of the Holy Spirit, who lives in you and was given to you by God? You do not belong to yourself, for God bought you with a high price. So you must honor God with your body. (NLT)

Problem 3 = Serving Jesus without love.

I Corinthians 13:1-3 If I could speak all the languages of earth and of angels, but didn't love others, I would only be a noisy gong or a clanging cymbal. If I had the gift of prophecy, and if I understood all of

God's secret plans and possessed all knowledge, and if I had such faith that I could move mountains, but didn't love others, I would be nothing. If I gave everything I have to the poor and even sacrificed my body, I could boast about it; but if I didn't love others, I would have gained nothing. (NLT)

Paul's solution = Genuinely love each other at church.

I Corinthians 13:4-7 Love is patient and kind. Love is not jealous or boastful or proud or rude. It does not demand its own way. It is not irritable, and it keeps no record of being wronged. It does not rejoice about injustice but rejoices whenever the truth wins out. Love never gives up, never loses faith, is always hopeful, and endures through every circumstance. (NLT)

LET'S APPLY IT!

1. Are there believers with whom you are in conflict rather than unity? The evidence of spiritual maturity is we seek to reconcile and work together.

    Matthew 5:23-24 "...if you are presenting a sacrifice at the altar in the Temple and you suddenly remember that someone has something against you, leave your sacrifice there at the altar. Go and be reconciled to that person. Then come and offer your sacrifice to God." (NLT)

2. You host the Holy Spirit. Your body is His temple. Are you honoring Him with your sex life?

3. Are you serving Jesus out of love for people? Decide to love the people of your church with genuine love!

    I John 4:19 We love him because he first loved us.

2 CORINTHIANS

📖 **Book:** 47 of 66

🔊 **Author:** The Apostle Paul. In this book, Paul gets more personal than any other. At one point he lists all the trials he has been through for the sake of Christ (2 Corinthians 11:23-28).

📝 **Type of Literature:** Epistle. 2 Corinthians is a follow-up letter to the Christians in the city of Corinth.

📅 **Date of Writing:** Paul writes this letter in A.D. 55–56, about a year after the completion of 1 Corinthians.

BIG IDEA OF 2 CORINTHIANS:
Christ gives us a new way of being human.

🔑 **Key verse:**
2 Corinthians 5:17 ...anyone who belongs to Christ has become a new person. The old life is gone; a new life has begun! (NLT)

5 WAYS PAUL SAYS WE ARE DIFFERENT IN CHRIST:

1. We are different in the way we handle trouble.

2 Corinthians 1:3-5 All praise to God, the Father of our Lord Jesus Christ. God is our merciful Father and the source of all comfort. He comforts us in all our troubles so that we can comfort others. When they are troubled, we will be able to give them the same comfort God has given us. For the more we suffer for Christ, the more God will shower us with his comfort through Christ. (NLT)

2 Corinthians 4:17-18 For our present troubles are small and won't last very long. Yet they produce for us a glory that vastly outweighs them and will last forever! (NLT)

2. We are different in our reason for living.

2 Corinthians 5:20 So we are Christ's ambassadors; God is making his appeal through us. We speak for Christ when we plead, "Come back to God!" (NLT)

3. We are different in how we choose a spouse.

2 Corinthians 6:14-16 Don't team up with those who are unbelievers. How can righteousness be a partner with wickedness? How can light live with darkness? What harmony can there be between Christ and the devil? How can a believer be a partner with an unbeliever? And what union can there be between God's temple and idols... (NLT)

4. We are different in how we use our money.

2 Corinthians 8:7 Since you excel in so many ways—in your faith, your gifted speakers, your knowledge, your enthusiasm, and your love from us—I want you to excel also in this gracious act of giving. (NLT)

2 Corinthians 9:6-8 Remember this—a farmer who plants only a few seeds will get a small crop. But the one who plants generously will get a generous crop. You must each decide in your heart how much to give. And don't give reluctantly or in response to pressure. "For God loves a person who gives cheerfully." And God will generously provide all you need. Then you will always have everything you need and plenty left over to share with others. (NLT)

5. We are different in what we put in our minds.

2 Corinthians 10:5 ...casting down arguments and every high thing that exalts itself against the knowledge of God, bringing every thought into captivity to the obedience of Christ.

LET'S APPLY IT!

1. Which of those 5 ways did the Holy Spirit speak directly to you about today? Will you embrace His new way of living?

2. Ask yourself: Am I truly living differently than the world? If you were to honestly examine your life, is there evidence you are a Christian at all?

   2 Corinthians 13:5 Examine yourselves as to whether you are in the faith. Test yourselves. Do you not know yourselves, that Jesus Christ is in you? –unless indeed you are disqualified.

Book: 48 of 66

Author: The Apostle Paul.

Type of Literature: Epistle. Galatians is a letter from Paul to the churches in the area of Galatia (Galatians 1:2).

Audience: Galatia was a region in what is now Turkey; Ankara, the capital of modern Turkey, was once a major Galatian city (Ancyra). The Book of Acts says that Paul traveled through "south Galatia" including the cities of Pisidian Antioch, Iconium, Lystra, and Derbe. Paul also visited Perga and Attalia in the region of Pamphylia on the Mediterranean coast (Acts 13-16).

Setting: Paul probably wrote this letter from his home city of Antioch, Syria.

Date of Writing: Galatians is one of the first New Testament books to be written, composed sometime around 49 A.D. (about 20 years after Jesus' resurrection).

BIG IDEA OF GALATIANS:
Be free! Exchange law (human effort) for Spirit-filled living.

Galatians 3:1-3 Oh, foolish Galatians! Who has cast an evil spell on you? For the meaning of Jesus Christ's death was made as clear to you as if you had seen a picture of his death on the cross. Let me ask you this one question: Did you receive the Holy Spirit by obeying the law (rules) of Moses? Of course not! You received the Spirit because you <u>believed the message you heard about Christ</u>. How foolish can you be? <u>After starting your new lives in the Spirit, why are you now trying to become perfect by your own human effort</u>? (NLT)

- We become saved by faith, and we become changed by faith.

Paul's Teaching on Self-effort vs. Spirit-filled living

Galatians 3:25 ...now that the way of faith has come, we no longer need the law [self-effort]. (NLT)

- Now that we have faith in Christ, we don't need to try to be better people. We seek the Lord and He makes us better people.

Galatians 5:1 So Christ has truly set us free. Now make sure that you stay free, and don't get tied up again in slavery to the law [self-effort]. (NLT)

- Christ forgave you and freed you from sin. Don't go back to trying to free yourself from sin.

Galatians 5:4 For if you are trying to make yourselves right with God by keeping the law, you have been cut off from Christ! You have fallen away from God's grace. (NLT)

- If you go back to self-effort, you are rejecting true Christianity.

MILLION DOLLAR QUESTION: IF I AM NOT SUPPOSED TO TRY TO CHANGE IN MY OWN STRENGTH, WHAT DO I DO?

Galatians 5:16 So I say, <u>let the Holy Spirit guide your lives</u>. THEN you won't be doing what your sinful nature craves. (NLT)

1. Yield your life every moment to the Holy Spirit. Don't try to be different in your own strength.

Galatians 5:17a The <u>sinful nature [self-effort/flesh] wants to do evil</u>, which is just the opposite of what the Spirit wants. And <u>the Spirit gives us desires</u> that are the opposite of what the sinful nature desires. (NLT)

2. Holy Spirit will give you the desire to do the right things. Your flesh won't.

Galatians 5:17b-18 These two forces are constantly fighting each other, so you are <u>not free to carry out your good intentions</u>. But when you are <u>directed by the Spirit</u>, you are not under obligation to the law of Moses. (NLT)

3. **Daily yield to Holy Spirit. Don't try to do anything in your own strength.**

Galatians 5:19-21 When you follow the desires of your sinful nature [self-effort/flesh], the results are very clear: sexual immorality, impurity, lustful pleasures, idolatry, sorcery, hostility, quarreling, jealousy, outbursts of anger, selfish ambition, dissension, division, envy, drunkenness, wild parties, and other sins like these. Let me tell you again, as I have before, that anyone living that sort of life will not inherit the Kingdom of God. (NLT)

4. **The result of our self-effort is always disastrous. We cannot win a spiritual war in our flesh.**

Galatians 5:22-23 But <u>the Holy Spirit produces</u> this kind of fruit in our lives: love, joy, peace, patience, kindness, goodness, faithfulness, gentleness, and self-control. <u>There is no law against these things</u>! (NLT)

5. **When we are controlled by the Holy Spirit, we naturally do the right things and don't need rules.**

Galatians 5:24-25 Those who belong to Christ Jesus have nailed the passions and desires of their sinful nature to his cross and crucified them there. Since we are living by the Spirit, <u>let us follow the Spirit's leading in every part of our lives</u>. (NLT)

6. **Follow the leading of the Holy Spirit. This is how we change!**

LET'S APPLY IT!

- Are you seeking to follow Jesus in the flesh?

- Are you using self-effort to try to change rather than Holy Spirit's strength?

- What if you rejected trying to be a better person and instead every day (every moment) yielded yourself to the Holy Spirit?

EPHESIANS

📖 **Book:** 49 of 66

🕵 **Author:** The Apostle Paul.

✍️ **Type of Literature:** Epistle. Ephesians is a letter from Paul to the church in Ephesus and the surrounding area.

🌐 **Audience:** On Paul's 2nd missionary journey, he and the pastoral couple Aquila & Priscilla (Acts 18:18-19) came to Ephesus and preached. On Paul's 3rd missionary journey, he took the few believers there and started a church and discipled them for two years (Acts 19:10). Eventually Timothy pastored the church here (1 Timothy 1:3). The Apostle John & Jesus' mother Mary eventually died here.

🎬 **Setting:** Paul is in a Roman prison writing to those he has led to Christ in Ephesus. Ephesus was a cult city of 250,000 people. Women ruled over men in this culture and the legend of Amazonian women comes from here. The temple of Artemis (Greek fertility goddess) was located here and was larger and more magnificent than the pyramids of Egypt. It was one of the Seven Wonders of the Ancient World.

📅 **Date of Writing:** Around 60-63 A.D.

BIG IDEA OF EPHESIANS:
BE RICH! Understanding your blessings and responsibilities in Christ.

Chapter 1-3 A believer's wealth.

Ephesians 1:3 All praise to God, the Father of our Lord Jesus Christ, who has blessed us with every spiritual blessing in the heavenly realms because we are united with Christ. (NLT)

Our Riches in Christ:
- Blessed (vs. 3)
- Chosen (vs. 4)
- Made holy (vs. 4)
- Without blame (vs. 4)
- Adopted (vs. 5)
- Accepted (vs. 6)
- Beloved (vs. 6)
- Redeemed (vs. 7)
- Forgiven (vs. 7)
- Graced/favored (vs. 7)
- Enlightened with wisdom (vs. 8-9)
- Given an inheritance (vs. 11)
- Sealed with the Holy Spirit (vs. 13)
- Guaranteed the inheritance of Heaven (vs. 14)

How did we get these things? G. R. A. C. E.
- **G**od's
- **R**iches
- **A**t
- **C**hrist's
- **E**xpense

Ephesians 2:8-9 God saved you by his grace when you believed. And you can't take credit for this; it is a gift from God. Salvation is not a reward for the good things we have done, so none of us can boast about it. (NLT)

Chapters 4-5 A believer's walk.

Ephesians 4:1 I, therefore, the prisoner of the Lord, beseech you to walk worthy of the calling with which you were called.

- **HOW DO WE WALK WORTHY?**
  Listen to your leaders.

  Ephesians 4:11-12 Now these are the gifts Christ gave to the church: the apostles, the prophets, the evangelists, and the pastors and teachers. Their responsibility is to equip God's people to do his work and build up the church, the body of Christ. (NLT)

Ephesians 5:1-2 Therefore be imitators of God as dear children. And walk in love, as Christ also has loved us and given Himself for us...

- **HOW DO WE WALK IN LOVE?**

  Ephesians 5:21 ...further, submit to one another out of reverence for Christ. (NLT)

  Walk in love = mutual submission.

  Ephesians 5:22 For wives, this means submit to your husbands as to the Lord. (NLT)

  Walk in love = Wives, put your husbands first.

  Ephesians 5:25 For husbands, this means love your wives, just as Christ loved the church. He gave up his life for her... (NLT)

  Walk in love = Husbands, put your wives first.

  Ephesians 6:4 Fathers [parents], do not provoke your children to anger by the way you treat them. Rather, bring them up with the discipline and instruction that comes from the Lord. (NLT)

  Walk in love = Parents, lead your kids to love Jesus.

Chapter 6 - A believer's war.

Ephesians 6:10-18 A final word: Be strong in the Lord and in his mighty power. Put on all of God's armor so that you will be able to stand firm against all strategies of the devil. For we are not fighting against flesh-and-blood enemies, but against evil rulers and authorities of the unseen world, against mighty powers in this dark world, and against evil spirits in the heavenly places. Therefore, put on every piece of God's armor so you will be able to resist the enemy in the time of evil. Then after the battle you will still be standing firm. Stand your ground, putting on the belt of truth and the body armor of God's righteousness. For shoes, put on the peace that comes from the Good News so that *you will be fully prepared. In addition to all of these, <u>hold up the shield of faith</u> to stop the fiery arrows of the devil. <u>Put on salvation as your helmet</u>, and <u>take the sword of the Spirit</u>, which is the word of God. Pray in the Spirit at all times and on every occasion... (NLT)*

LET'S APPLY IT!

1. WEALTH - Did you forget how rich you are? Why are you so worried and afraid?

   Luke 12:32 "Do not fear, little flock, for it is your Father's good pleasure to give you the kingdom."

2. WALK - Will you walk worthy of your calling?

   - Listen to your leaders.

   - Love your spouse sacrificially.

   - Lead your kids to love Jesus.

3. WAR - Will you put on your armor and win your war?

PHILIPPIANS

📖 **Book:** 50 of 66

🧑 **Author:** The Apostle Paul.

✏️ **Type of Literature:** Epistle. Philippians is a letter Paul wrote to a small group of Christians in Philippi.

📅 **Date of Writing:** The Book of Philippians was written in approximately A.D. 60-62

🎬 **Setting:** The Apostle Paul is in a Roman prison doing the best he can to encourage Christians in Philippi.

🌐 **Audience:** This book is written to believers in the Roman colony of Philippi. Philippi was a smaller military outpost in northern Greece (pop. 10k), inhabited primarily by retired military and political figures that were given land by the Roman government. Paul started the church here during his second missionary journey around A.D. 49 (Acts 16). This was the first church ever established in Europe.

BIG IDEA OF PHILIPPIANS:
Joy in a jail cell.

🔑 **Key verse:**
Philippians 4:4 Rejoice in the Lord ALWAYS. Again I will say, rejoice!

Chapter 1 - You're gonna make it!

Philippians 1:6 ...being confident of this very thing, that He who has begun a good work in you will complete it until the day of Jesus Christ.

Isaiah 64:8 We are the clay, and you are the potter. We all are formed by your hand. (NLT)

Chapter 2 - Jesus is our better model.

Philippians 2:5-11 <u>Let this mind be in you</u> which was also in Christ Jesus, who, being in the form of God, did not consider it robbery to be equal with God, but made Himself of no reputation, taking the form of a bondservant, and coming in the likeness of men. And being found in appearance as a man, He humbled Himself and became obedient to the point of death, even the death of the cross. Therefore God also has highly exalted Him and given Him the name which is above every name, that at <u>the name of Jesus every knee should bow</u>, of those in heaven, and of those on earth, and of those under the earth, and that every tongue should confess that Jesus Christ is Lord, to the glory of God the Father.

Chapter 3 - Forget the past, keep moving forward!

Philippians 3:13-14 ...<u>one thing I do, forgetting those things which are behind</u> and <u>reaching forward</u> to those things which are ahead, I press toward the goal for the prize of the upward call of God in Christ Jesus.

Chapter 4 - Keep changing your mind!

Philippians 4:6-8 Be <u>anxious</u> for nothing, but in everything by <u>prayer</u> and supplication, with thanksgiving, let your requests be made known to God; and the <u>peace of God</u>, which surpasses all understanding, will guard your hearts and minds through Christ Jesus. Finally, brethren, whatever things are true, whatever things are noble, whatever things are just, whatever things are pure, whatever things are lovely, whatever things are of good report, if there is any virtue and if there is anything praiseworthy–<u>meditate on these things</u>.

LET'S APPLY IT!

Which of those 4 thoughts from Paul did you need to hear most today?

- Christ is committed to completing His work in you. Let Him work!

- Jesus is only healthy model for living. Keep kneeling at His feet!

- Forget the past and keep moving forward! He has reward for you.

- Keep your mind focused on the good. Filter out the garbage.

  Psalms 16:11 ...In Your presence is fullness of joy...

COLOSSIANS

📑 **Book:** 51 of 66

🧑 **Author:** The Apostle Paul.

✍️ **Type of Literature:** Epistle. Colossians is a letter written to the believers in the city of Colossae.

🌐 **Audience:** The city of Colossae was about 100 miles east of Ephesus in modern-day Turkey. The gospel may have reached this city during Paul's two years in Ephesus (Acts 19:10).

🗂️ **Setting:** The Apostle Paul wrote this letter while under house arrest in Rome.

📅 **Date of Writing:** Around A.D. 60-62.

BIG IDEA OF COLOSSIANS:
Only Jesus makes us complete.

Colossians 2:8-10 <u>*Beware lest anyone cheat you*</u> *through philosophy and empty deceit, according to the tradition of men, according to the basic principles of the world, and not according to Christ. For in Him dwells all the fullness of the Godhead bodily; and* <u>*you are complete in Him,*</u> *who is the head of all principality and power.*

LET'S APPLY IT!
If only Jesus makes us complete…

1. Keep thanking Jesus for His miracles!

Colossians 1:13-18 For he has <u>*rescued us from the kingdom of darkness*</u> *and transferred us into the Kingdom of his dear Son, who* <u>*purchased our freedom*</u> *and* <u>*forgave our sins*</u>. *…for* <u>*through him God created everything*</u> *in the heavenly realms and on earth. He made the things we can see and the things we can't see—such as thrones, kingdoms, rulers, and authorities in the unseen world.* <u>*Everything was created through him and for him*</u>. *He existed before anything else, and* <u>*he holds all creation together*</u>. <u>*Christ is also the head of the church,*</u> *which is his body… (NLT)*

Let's thank Jesus for what He has done!

- He delivered us from darkness. (vs. 13)
- He purchased our freedom. (vs. 14)
- He forgave our sins. (vs. 14)
- He created us. (vs. 15-16)
- He holds us together. (vs. 17)
- He leads us. (vs. 17-18)

2. Keep digging deeper into the truths of Scripture.

Colossians 2:6-7 ...now just as you accepted Christ Jesus as your Lord, you must continue to follow him. <u>Let your roots grow down into him</u>, and let your lives be built on him. Then your faith will grow strong <u>in the truth you were taught</u>... (NLT)

- Spiritual growth cannot exist without spiritual knowledge.

3. Keep seeking the goals of Jesus.

Colossians 3:1-2 If then you were raised with Christ, <u>seek those things which are above</u>, where Christ is, sitting at the right hand of God. <u>Set your mind on things above, NOT on things on the earth</u>.

What am I living for? Heaven's goals or earthly goals?

Is there any part of my day/week where I am:
- Using my time for heaven's purposes?
- Pointing my kids to embrace Jesus' ways?
- Using my money & talents to advance Jesus' name?
- Orbiting my family around Christ?
- Making Jesus the center of my marriage or dating relationship?

4. **Keep reaching the lost for Jesus.**

    Colossians 4:3 ...praying also for us, that God would open to us a door for the word, <u>to speak the mystery of Christ</u>...

    We exist to help as many people as we can cross the line of faith and follow Jesus.

1 & 2 THESSALONIANS

📖 **Books:** 52 & 53 of 66

👤 **Author:** The Apostle Paul.

✍️ **Type of Literature:** Epistles. 1 & 2 Thessalonians are two letters written to the believers in the city of Thessalonica.

🌐 **Audience:** The city of Thessalonica was located in Northern Greece. Paul came to Thessalonica from Philippi on his second missionary journey (Acts 17). He preached in the city's synagogue for about 3 weeks and then established a small, mostly Gentile church there (1 Thessalonians 1:9). Paul then faced persecution from a violent mob and fled the city. The believers here faced constant persecution from unbelievers and needed continual encouragement.

📅 **Date of Writing:** The Book of 1 Thessalonians was written around 50 A.D., and 2 Thessalonians around 51 or 52 A.D. These were some of the first New Testament books written.

BIG IDEA OF 1 THESSALONIANS:
Jesus is returning - look for the Rapture!

Rapture = Jesus takes His Church (His bride) UP out of this world to Heaven. Greek word *Harpazo* = caught up, catch up or away, taken by force, to pluck, or to pull.

I Thessalonians 1:10 ...wait for His Son from heaven, whom He raised from the dead, even Jesus who <u>delivers us from the wrath to come</u>.

• Jesus will deliver His Church from the coming wrath of the seven-year tribulation.

I Thessalonians 5:2, 9 For you yourselves know full well that the day of the Lord will come just like a thief in the night... For God has not destined us for wrath, but for obtaining salvation through our Lord Jesus Christ... (NASB 1995)

- God did not plan for His people to endure God's wrath but instead be saved from it through Christ.

I Thessalonians 4:13-16 And now, dear brothers and sisters, we want you to know what will happen to the believers who have died so you will not grieve like people who have no hope. For since we believe that Jesus died and was raised to life again, we also believe that when Jesus returns, God will bring back with him the believers who have died. [Souls] We tell you this directly from the Lord: We who are still living when the Lord returns will not meet him ahead of those who have died. For the Lord himself will come down from heaven with a commanding shout, with the voice of the archangel, and with the trumpet call of God. First, the believers who have died will rise from their graves. (NLT)

- At the moment of the Rapture, God will resurrect all the believers who have died and reconnect them with new glorified bodies.

I Thessalonians 4:17-18 Then, together with them, we who are still alive and remain on the earth will be <u>caught up</u> [harpazo] in the clouds to meet the Lord in the air. Then we will be with the Lord forever. So encourage each other with these words. (NLT)

- After the dead believers rise, we who are still alive will be "caught up" (raptured) to meet the Lord in the air and given new glorified bodies as well.

    Cross reference: *I Corinthians 15:51-53*

LET'S APPLY IT!

- Watch! Be ready!

    I Thessalonians 5:1-6 Now concerning how and when all this will happen, dear brothers and sisters, we don't really need to write you. For you know quite well that the day of the Lord's return <u>will come unexpectedly, like a thief in the night</u>. When people are saying, "Everything is peaceful and secure," then disaster will fall on them as suddenly as a pregnant woman's labor pains begin. And there will be no escape. But you aren't in the dark about these *things, dear brothers and sisters, and <u>you won't be surprised when the day of the Lord comes like a thief</u>. For you are all children of the light and of the day; we don't belong to darkness and night. <u>So be on your guard</u>, not asleep like the others. <u>Stay alert and be clearheaded</u>. (NLT)*

BIG IDEA OF 2 THESSALONIANS:
Jesus is returning. Look for signs of the Antichrist!

2 Thessalonians 2:1-4 Now, dear brothers and sisters, let us clarify some things about the coming of our Lord Jesus Christ and how we will be gathered to meet him…For that day will not come until there is <u>a great rebellion against God and the man of lawlessness is revealed</u>—the one who <u>brings destruction</u>. He will <u>exalt himself and defy everything that people call god and every object of worship</u>. <u>He will even sit in the temple of God, claiming that he himself is God</u>. (NLT)

The Antichrist will:

- Lead a rebellion against God

- Bring a massive amount of destruction to the world (see also Daniel 8:24)

- Sit in the Temple in Jerusalem and claim to be God (see also Daniel 9:27)

2 Thessalonians 2:8-12 …the man of lawlessness will be revealed, but the <u>Lord Jesus will slay him with the breath of his mouth and destroy him</u> by the splendor of his coming. <u>This man will come to do the work of Satan with counterfeit power and signs and miracles. He will use every kind of evil deception to fool those on their way to destruction, because they refuse to love and accept the truth that would save them</u>. So God will cause them to be greatly deceived, and they will believe these lies. Then they will be condemned for enjoying evil rather than believing the truth. (NLT)

The Antichrist will:

- Do the works of Satan

- Perform counterfeit miracles

- Deceive unbelievers

- Be destroyed by Jesus at the battle of Armageddon (see also Revelation 19:11-21)

LET'S APPLY IT!

- Stand firm. Stay in the Word!

  2 Thessalonians 2:15 With all these things in mind, dear brothers and sisters, stand firm and keep a strong grip on the teaching we passed on to you both in person and by letter. (NLT)

1 & 2 TIMOTHY

Books: 54 & 55 of 66

Author: The Apostle Paul.

Type of Literature: Epistles. I & 2 Timothy are letters from Paul to Timothy, who was the pastor in Ephesus. These letters are known as "Pastoral Epistles" or wisdom on how to pastor.

Audience: Timothy was from Lystra (modern-day Turkey). He was the son of a Greek father and Jewish mother. Timothy's mom and grandmother were believers (2 Timothy 1:5). He was led to Christ by Paul (1 Timothy 1:2).

Setting: Paul wrote these letters to encourage Timothy to stay faithfully serving Jesus and leading the church. Timothy at one point led Mary the mother of Jesus and the Apostle John. Both attended his church.

Date of Writing: 1 Timothy was written in 62-65 A.D., probably from Macedonia (northern Greece), and 2 Timothy was the last letter Paul wrote around 67 A.D., right before his death in Rome.

BIG IDEA OF 1 & 2 TIMOTHY:
How to step up and lead!

- In your church. The church needs Christlike leaders.

- In your home. You are the pastors & priests of your home.

1. **Cling to Christ. Nothing matters more than your relationship with Jesus!**

   I Timothy 1:18-19 Timothy, my son, here are my instructions for you, based on the prophetic words spoken about you earlier. May they help you fight well in the Lord's battles. Cling to your faith in Christ, and keep your conscience clear. For some people have deliberately violated their consciences; as a result, their faith has been shipwrecked. (NLT)

2. Character. Be a person of integrity.

I Timothy 3:1-5 This is a trustworthy saying: "If someone aspires to be a church leader, he desires an honorable position." So a church leader must be a man [or woman] whose life is above reproach. He must be faithful to his wife [spouse]. He must exercise self-control, live wisely, and have a good reputation. He must enjoy having guests in his home, and he must be able to teach. He must not be a heavy drinker or be violent. He must be gentle, not quarrelsome, and not love money. He must manage his own family well, having children who respect and obey him. For if a man cannot manage his own household, how can he take care of God's church? (NLT)

3. Competence. Set a good example in life and teaching.

2 Timothy 4:11-12 Teach these things and insist that everyone learn them. Don't let anyone think less of you because you are young. Be an example to all believers in what you say, in the way you live, in your love, your faith, and your purity. (NLT)

2 Timothy 2:15 Be diligent to present yourself approved to God as a worker who does not need to be ashamed, accurately handling the word of truth. (NASB)

4. Contentment. Reject consumerism and embrace giving.

- Consumerism = an obsession with stuff and status more than Jesus.

- Contentment = living joyfully and at peace with whatever God gives you knowing God is good and wants to give good gifts to His children.

- Giving = knowing all you have is from God, so you freely use what He gives you for His purposes.

I Timothy 6:6, 9-10 Yet true godliness with <u>contentment is itself great wealth</u>...people who long to be rich fall into temptation and are trapped by many foolish and harmful desires that plunge them into ruin and destruction. For the love of money is the root of all kinds of evil. And some people, craving money, have wandered from the true faith and pierced themselves with many sorrows. (NLT)

I Timothy 6:17-18 Teach those who are rich in this world not to be proud and not to trust in their money, which is so unreliable. Their trust should be in God, who richly gives us all we need for our enjoyment. <u>Tell them to use their money to do good</u>. They should be rich in good works and <u>generous</u> to those in need, always being ready to <u>share</u> with others. (NLT)

5. Commitment. Never give up. Stay faithful. Jesus is worth it!

2 Timothy 2:3 <u>Endure suffering</u> along with me, as a good soldier of Christ Jesus. (NLT)

2 Timothy 4:5-8 <u>Don't be afraid of suffering for the Lord</u>. Work at telling others the Good News, and fully carry out the ministry God has given you. As for me, my life has already been poured out as an offering to God. The time of my death is near. I have fought the good fight, I have finished the race, and <u>I have remained faithful</u>. And now the prize awaits me—the crown of righteousness, which the Lord, the righteous Judge, will give me on the day of his return. And the prize is not just for me but for all who eagerly look forward to his appearing. (NLT)

LET'S APPLY IT!

1. God wants you to step up & lead in your home & church! Will you step up and lead?

2. Which of these did Holy Spirit speak directly to you about today?

- Cling to Christ

- Character

- Competence

- Contentment

- Commitment

TITUS

📖 **Book:** 56 of 66

🎧 **Author:** The Apostle Paul.

📝 **Type of Literature:** Epistle. Titus is a letter from Paul.

📅 **Date of Writing:** Titus was written approximately A.D. 64 from Rome.

🌐 **Audience:** Titus was written to a church planter named Titus who was sent by Paul to start churches on the island of Crete.

BIG IDEA OF TITUS:
Pastor manual for starting healthy churches and raising up godly leaders.

🔑 **Key verse:**
Titus 1:5 For this reason I left you in Crete, that you should <u>set in order the things</u> that are lacking, and <u>appoint elders</u> in <u>every city</u>...

3 theological ideas are implied in this verse:

Titus 1:5 <u>Set in order</u> the things that are lacking...

1. A healthy church must set up a healthy structure for growth.

Philippians 2:2 ...UNITED in spirit, intent on ONE purpose. (NASB)

Titus 1:5 ...in every city...

2. A healthy church starts more churches.

Titus 1:5 ...and appoint elders...

3. A healthy church has a game plan to train up godly leaders to pastor and lead churches.

LET'S APPLY IT!

How can you contribute to the mission of starting and supporting healthy churches in every town?

1. GO - on mission trips or on to leadership.

2. GIVE - Not everyone can go, but everyone can give.

    Titus 3:14 ...do good by meeting the urgent needs of others; then they will not be unproductive. (NLT)

    Romans 15:26 ...the believers in Macedonia and Achaia have eagerly taken up an offering for the poor among the believers in Jerusalem. (NLT)

    Romans 5:8 But God demonstrates His own love toward us, in that while we were still sinners, Christ died for us.

PHILEMON

Book: 57 of 66

Author: The Apostle Paul.

Type of Literature: Epistle. Philemon is a letter from Paul.

Date of Writing: Philemon was written approximately A.D. 60-62 from Rome.

Audience: Philemon was written to a wealthy Christian named Philemon who had a church in his house in the city of Colossae (located in modern-day southwestern Turkey).

BIG IDEA OF PHILEMON:
Reconcile! Brothers in Christ work together and forgive and love each other!

The Back Story:
Onesimus was a slave who rebelled and ran away from his master Philemon. Onesimus fled to Rome where he met Paul and became a Christian. Paul then sent Onesimus back to Philemon, along with this letter which encouraged Philemon to forgive Onesimus for running away and to reconcile with him and release him. Tradition says that Onesimus became a leader in the church that met in Philemon's house.

The Issue of Slavery:
Sometimes people try to criticize the Bible and say it "approves of slavery," but the Book of Philemon throws a hand grenade on the practice of slavery and encourages Christian brotherhood, freedom of slaves, and reconciliation and forgiveness between slaves and slave owners.

Key verse:
Philemon 1:12 I am sending him back. You therefore <u>receive</u> him...

1. **Reconcile. I know he (Onesimus) probably wronged you (and you wronged him), but welcome him back.**

Romans 15:7 *Therefore welcome one another as Christ has welcomed you, for the glory of God. (ESV)*

Matthew 5:23-24 *"So if you are presenting a sacrifice at the altar in the Temple and you suddenly remember that someone has something against you, leave your sacrifice there at the altar. Go and be reconciled to that person. Then come and offer your sacrifice to God." (NLT)*

Philemon 1:15-16 *...you might <u>receive him forever,</u> no longer as a slave but more than a slave—<u>a beloved brother</u>...*

2. **The church is a family. We are brothers and sisters (not slaves) in Christ, so lovingly work together.**

    Hebrews 10:19 *And now we are brothers and sisters in God's family because of the blood of Jesus... (TPT)*

    Romans 12:10 *Be kindly affectionate to one another with brotherly love...*

Philemon 1:17-18 *If then you count me as a partner, <u>receive him as you would me</u>. But if he has wronged you or owes anything, put that on my account.*

3. **Forgive each other and work together like you would with the Apostle Paul himself.**

    Ephesians 4:32 *...be kind to each other, tenderhearted, forgiving one another, just as God through Christ has forgiven you. (NLT)*

    Philippians 1:27 *...stand fast in ONE spirit, with ONE mind <u>striving together</u> for the faith of the gospel...*

LET'S APPLY IT!

- Will you seek to make amends with people you have wronged because you love Jesus?

- Will you forgive the people who wronged you because Jesus has forgiven you?

- Will you work as one Church for the good of the gospel?

Book: 58 of 66

Author: Unknown. The book was already widely circulated among the churches by 95 A.D. and quoted by many early church pastors, but no one knows for sure who wrote it. Suggestions have included Paul, Apollos, Peter, Silas, Barnabas, and Aquila & Priscilla.

Type of Literature: Epistle. Hebrews is a letter to the Jewish Christians throughout the Roman Empire.

Date of Writing: Approximately 65 A.D. Since the book is to Jewish Christians and there is no mention of the destruction of Jerusalem in 70 A.D., it was probably written before then.

Audience: Dr. Walter Martin, author & theologian jokingly wrote that, "The book of Hebrews was written by a Hebrew to other Hebrews telling the Hebrews to stop acting like Hebrews." This idea is not far from the reality. Many Jewish Christians were sliding back into the rituals of Judaism in order to escape persecution from other Jews. This letter is an explanation as to why Jesus is better than Judaism and to stay faithful to Christ in the face of persecution.

BIG IDEA OF HEBREWS:
Jesus is better!

1. Jesus is better than the prophets.

Hebrews 1:1-2 Long ago God spoke many times and in many ways to our ancestors through the prophets. And now in these final days, he has spoken to us through his Son. God promised everything to the Son as an inheritance, and through the Son he created the universe. (NLT)

2. Jesus is better than angels.

Hebrews 1:3-4 The Son radiates God's own glory and expresses the very character of God, and he sustains everything by the mighty *power of his command. When he had cleansed us from our sins, he sat down in the place of honor at the right hand of the majestic God in heaven. <u>This shows that the Son is far greater than the angels</u>... (NLT)*

3. Jesus is better than the Old Testament Law.

Hebrews 8:6 ...now Jesus, our High Priest, has been given a ministry that is far superior to the old priesthood, for he is the one who mediates for us <u>a far better covenant with God</u>, based on better promises. (NLT)

Hebrews 8:10, 12 ...this is the new covenant I will make with the people of Israel on that day, says the LORD: I will put my laws in their minds, and I will write them on their hearts. I will be their God, and they will be my people... I will forgive their wickedness, and I will never again remember their sins. (NLT)

4. Jesus is better than Old Testament sacrifices.

Hebrews 10:4; 19-22 ...<u>it is not possible for the blood of bulls and goats to take away sins</u>. And so, dear brothers and sisters, we can boldly enter heaven's Most Holy Place because of the blood of Jesus. By his death, Jesus opened a new and life-giving way... <u>For our guilty consciences have been sprinkled with Christ's blood to make us clean</u>, and our bodies have been washed with pure water.

LET'S APPLY IT!

1. Jesus is better than sex.

    Hebrews 13:4 Let marriage be held in honor among all, and let the marriage bed be undefiled, for God will judge the sexually immoral and adulterous. (ESV)

2. Jesus is better than wealth.

   Hebrews 13:16 Do not neglect to do good and to <u>share what you have</u>, for such sacrifices are pleasing to God. (ESV)

   Hebrews 13:16 Do not neglect to do good, to contribute [to <u>the needy of the church as an expression of fellowship</u>], for such sacrifices are <u>ALWAYS pleasing to God</u>. (AMP)

3. Jesus is better than all other relationships.

   Hebrews 13:5 ..."I will never leave you nor forsake you..."

JAMES

📖 **Book:** 59 of 66

👤 **Author:** James, who was a half-brother of Jesus (Mt. 13:55; Mk. 6:3). James was not a disciple of Jesus until after the resurrection (Acts 1:14; 1 Corinthians 15:7; Galatians 1:19). He became one of the key leaders of the Jerusalem church, along with Peter and John (Galatians 2:9), and was stoned to death in 62 A.D. for his faith in Christ according to the Jewish historian Josephus.

✏️ **Type of Literature:** Epistle. James is a letter.

📅 **Date of Writing:** The Book of James is probably the first book written in the entire New Testament. James wrote maybe as early as 45 A.D., only 15 years after the resurrection of Jesus.

🌐 **Audience:** James is written "to the twelve tribes"–Jewish believers scattered abroad" (James 1:1). Basically, James wrote to Jewish Christians scattered throughout the Roman Empire and beyond.

BIG IDEA OF JAMES:
Do something with your faith!

The Hebrew word for faith - *emunah* - is a VERB and implies action. *Emunah* is often translated as "faith" or "belief" in English, however its meaning is closer to "active trust". It is a verb that implies doing, not just knowing.

Example:

- "I believe in Jesus" = knowing faith

- "I follow Jesus" = active faith

🔑 **Key Verse:**
James 2:17 ...faith by itself, if it does not have works, is dead.

- The evidence that faith is alive is that it produces actions.

- Jesus' grace is the engine. For by grace you have been saved (Ephesians 2:8-9).

- Faith is the first train car. We have been made right in God's sight by faith (Romans 5:1).

- Works are the rest of the train cars. They naturally follow God's grace and our faith.

4 ACTIONS THAT OUR FAITH PRODUCES:

1. Faith patiently endures.

James 1:2-4 Dear brothers and sisters, when troubles of any kind come your way, consider it an opportunity for great joy. For you know that when your faith is tested, your endurance has a chance to grow. So let it grow, for when your endurance is fully developed, you will be perfect and complete, needing nothing. (NLT)

2. Faith graciously speaks.

James 3:8-10 But no man can tame the tongue. It is an unruly evil, full of deadly poison. With it we bless our God and Father, and with it we curse men, who have been made in the similitude of God. Out of the same mouth proceed blessing and cursing. My brethren, these things ought not to be so.

3. Faith earnestly prays.

James 5:16-18 ...The earnest prayer of a righteous person has great power and produces wonderful results. Elijah was as human as we are, and yet when he prayed earnestly that no rain would fall, none fell for three and a half years! Then, when he prayed again, the sky sent down rain and the earth began to yield its crops. (NLT)

4. Faith actively cares.

James 1:27 Pure and genuine religion in the sight of God the Father means <u>caring for orphans and widows in their distress</u> and refusing to let the world corrupt you. (NLT)

LET'S APPLY IT!

1. Genuine faith leads to actions. In what ways can you see active faith in your life?

2. Even salvation itself starts with a vocal "faith/action" step.

   Romans 10:9 ...that if you confess with your mouth the Lord Jesus and believe in your heart that God has raised Him from the dead, you will be saved.

1 & 2 PETER

Books: 60 & 61 of 66

Author: The Apostle Peter.

Type of Literature: Epistles. These books are letters Peter wrote from "Babylon" - a cryptic name for Rome.

I Peter 5:13 Your sister church here in Babylon sends you greetings, and so does my son Mark. (NLT)

Date of Writing: These letters were written toward the end of Peter's life. He wrote 1 Peter between 60-64 A.D. and 2 Peter around 65 A.D.

Audience: I Peter and 2 Peter are written to churches planted throughout the Roman Empire.

I Peter 1:1 ...To God's elect, exiles scattered throughout the provinces of Pontus, Galatia, Cappadocia, Asia and Bithynia... (NIV)

Setting: About 60 A.D. Christians in the Roman Empire entered into a 250-year period of severe persecution (tortured & killed for sport). He writes to encourage Christians to stay faithful to Christ in spite of the persecution. Peter dies shortly after 2 Peter is written; crucified upside down under the orders of the Emperor Nero.

BIG IDEA OF 1 PETER:
"Suffer well."

- Peter uses the verb "suffering" twelve times, and the noun for "suffering" four times.

Key Verses:

I Peter 4:12 Beloved, <u>do not think it strange concerning the fiery trial which is to try you, as though some strange thing happened to you</u>...

- **Suffering is normal for Christians.**

I Peter 4:13 ...but rejoice to the extent that you _partake of Christ's suffering_, that when His glory is revealed, you may also be glad with exceeding joy.

- **REJOICE! Suffering connects us to Jesus in ways other things can't.**

- **When suffering, we are drinking from the same cup as Christ Himself. We can't get closer to Jesus than that.**

  Matthew 20:23 "_You will indeed drink My cup_, and be baptized with the baptism that I am baptized with..."

I Peter 4:14 If you are reproached for the name of Christ, _blessed are you_, for the Spirit of glory and of God rests upon you. On their part He is blasphemed, but on your part He is glorified.

- **There is a special blessing on our lives when we suffer. Look for it!**

I Peter 4:15-16, 19 But let none of you suffer as a murderer, a thief, an evildoer, or as a busybody in other people's matters. Yet if anyone suffers as a Christian, let him not be ashamed, but let him glorify God in this matter. Therefore let those who _suffer according to the will of God_ commit their souls to Him in doing good, as to a faithful Creator.

- **Our response to suffering is to:**
  a. Accept suffering as the will of God.
  b. Commit our souls to Him!

ONE OF THE BIG IDEAS OF 2 PETER:
Look forward to Christ's coming Kingdom!

🔑 Key Verses:

2 Peter 3:10-14 But the day of the Lord will come as a thief in the night, in which the heavens will pass away with a great noise, and the elements will melt with fervent heat; both the earth and the works that are in it will be burned up. Therefore, since all these things will be dissolved, what manner of persons ought you to be in <u>holy conduct and godliness</u>, looking for and hastening the coming of the day of God, because of which the heavens will be dissolved, being on fire, and the elements will melt with fervent heat? Nevertheless we, according to His promise, look for new heavens and a new earth in which righteousness dwells. Therefore, beloved, <u>looking forward</u> to these things, <u>be diligent</u> to be found by Him in peace…

- ***Holy conduct and godliness* - We live "set apart" as we anticipate Christ's return.**

- ***Looking forward* - We look with eagerness to Christ's return.**

- ***Be diligent* - We labor to build Christ's kingdom as we wait for His return.**

LET'S APPLY IT!

- 1 Peter - In what area of your life are you suffering? _____. Don't lose your hope! Will you trust Christ though your pain?

  Isaiah 40:31 …those who hope in the LORD will renew their strength. They will soar on wings like eagles; they will run and not grow weary, they will walk and not be faint. (NIV)

- 2 Peter - Christ is coming soon! Are you ready to meet Him? Will you labor diligently in anticipation of His return?

1, 2 & 3 JOHN & JUDE

Books: 62, 63, 64 & 65 of 66

Authors:

- 1, 2 & 3 John were written by John, the youngest disciple of Jesus. John lived the longest of all the disciples and he also wrote the Gospel of John & the Book of Revelation.

- Jude was written by the half-brother of Jesus - Judas. The title of the book was shortened to Jude to not confuse people with the betrayer of Jesus (different Judas).

Type of Literature: Epistles. All four of these books were letters.

Date of Writing:

- 1, 2 & 3 John were all written between 85-95 A.D., near the end of John's life.

- Jude was written between 67-80 A.D. Jude is very connected to 2 Peter and the same language is used in both. Many theologians speculate that Jude borrowed some of his ideas from 2 Peter. Since Peter died around 67, Jude must have been written shortly after.

Audience:

- 1 John was written to an unspecified audience. Because John spent the end of his life in or near Turkey and wrote Revelation partially to the "seven churches" in Turkey, many believe these churches were his intended audience.

- 2 John was written to "the elect lady and her children" (2 John 1:1). Some theories on who this lady was include:

  a. The Bride of Christ - church universal.

  b. A very personal letter to one specific woman and her actual children.

  c. A female pastor and her congregation.

- 3 John was written to a man called "the beloved Gaius" (3 John 1:1) who must have been an early church leader.

- Jude probably had a specific church or group of churches in mind when he wrote "certain people have crept in unnoticed...ungodly people, who pervert the grace of our God into sensuality" (Jude 1:4, ESV). Also, Jude has many references to the Old Testament and to other Jewish literature, so his readers were probably Jewish Christians.

BIG IDEA OF 1 JOHN:
Walk in love. The word love appears 35 times in 1 John.

The Greek word John uses for love is *"agape,"* which means self-sacrificing love. It goes beyond emotion (*eros*) or friendship (*phileo*) all the way to sacrificing of self for the good of another. Like a soldier jumps on a grenade to save others or Jesus sacrifices Himself for our sins, *agape* love means sacrifice.

I John 4:7-11 Beloved [you are sacrificed for], let us love [sacrifice for] one another, for love [sacrificial] is of God; and everyone who loves [sacrifices] is born of God and knows God. He who does not love [sacrifice] does not know God, for God is love [a self-sacrificer]. In this the [sacrificial] love of God was manifested toward us, that God has sent His only begotten Son into the world, that we might live through Him. In this [sacrificial] love, not that we loved [were willing to sacrifice for] God, but that He loved [sacrificed for] us and sent His Son to be the propitiation for our sins. Beloved, [you are sacrifice for] if God so loved [sacrificed for] us, we also ought to love [sacrifice for] one another.

BIG IDEA OF 2 JOHN:
Walk in obedience.

2 John 1:6 This is love, that we walk according to His commandments. This is the commandment, that as you have heard from the beginning, you should walk in it.

BIG IDEA OF 3 JOHN:
Walk in truth.

3 John 1:4 I have no greater joy than to hear that my children walk in truth.

BIG IDEA OF JUDE:
Walk in purity/holiness.

Jude 1:4 ...certain men have crept in unnoticed, who long ago were marked out for this condemnation, ungodly men, who <u>*turn the grace of our God into lewdness and deny the only Lord God and our Lord Jesus Christ*</u>.

LET'S APPLY IT!

- 1 John - Embrace the self-sacrifice of God, but also self-sacrifice for others.

- 2 John - Embrace being a "fan of Jesus," but go on to obediently following Jesus.

- 3 John - Embrace the basics, but also dig into the deeper truth of Scripture.

- Jude - Embrace forgiveness, but also holiness.

REVELATION

📖 **Book:** 66 of 66

👤 **Author:** The Apostle John. He was the youngest & closest disciple of Jesus. He was probably 12 when he became a disciple and 15 at the time of Jesus' death. When John wrote Revelation he was an old man, and the emperor had tried to kill him by boiling him in oil. However, he survived and instead got exiled to the Roman prison island of Patmos.

✒️ **Type of Literature:** Revelation is the only New Testament book of prophecy.

🌐 **Audience:** Revelation was written for all believers (Revelation 1:3), but specifically chapters 2-3 address seven churches all located in modern Turkey. Each church is given a specific message from Jesus on what they are doing well and how to stay faithful to Christ.

📅 **Date of Writing:** This book contains the last words of the New Testament, written approximately 95 A.D.

⭐ **Two Special Notes:**

1) This book contains a blessing for all who read it or hear it read aloud.

   Revelation 1:3 Blessed is the one who reads aloud the words of this prophecy, and blessed are those who hear it and take to heart what is written in it, because the time is near. (NIV)

2) This book contains a curse for anyone who adds to or takes away from this book.

   Revelation 22:18-19 And I solemnly declare to everyone who hears the words of prophecy written in this book: If anyone adds anything to what is written here, God will add to that person the plagues described in this book. And if anyone removes any of the words from this book of prophecy, God will remove that person's share in the tree of life and in the holy city that are described in this book. (NLT)

BIG IDEA OF REVELATION:
A revealing of what is to come.

Revelation 1:1 This is a <u>revelation</u> from Jesus Christ, which God gave him to <u>show his servants the events that must soon take place</u>... (NLT)

🔑 Key Verses & Revelations:

1. **Nineteen worldwide plagues during the last seven years before Christ returns.**

   Revelation 9:20-21 ...the people who did not die in these plagues still <u>refused to repent of their evil deeds and turn to God</u>. They continued to worship demons and idols made of gold, silver, bronze, stone, and wood—idols that can neither see nor hear nor walk! <u>And they did not repent</u> of their murders or their witchcraft [pharmarkia in Greek = drugs + magic = recreational drug use] or their sexual immorality [pornea in Greek] or their thefts. (NLT)

   - God allows these plagues to give people nineteen last chances to turn to Christ and be saved.

     2 Peter 3:9 [God] is being patient for your sake. He does not want anyone to be destroyed, but wants everyone to repent. (NLT)

2. **Christ's Second Coming:**

   Revelation 19:11-16 Then I saw heaven opened, and a white horse was standing there. Its rider was named Faithful and True, for he judges fairly and wages a righteous war. His eyes were like flames of fire, and on his head were many crowns. A name was written on him that no one understood except himself. He wore a robe dipped in blood, and his title was the Word of God. The armies of heaven, dressed in the finest of pure white linen, followed him on white horses. From his mouth came a sharp sword to strike down the nations. He will rule them with an iron rod. He will release the fierce wrath of God, the Almighty, like juice flowing from a winepress. On his robe at his thigh was written this title: King of all kings and Lord of all lords. (NLT)

3. The Final Judgment:

Revelation 20:11-15 And I saw a great white throne and the one sitting on it. The earth and sky fled from his presence, but they found no place to hide. I saw the dead, both great and small, standing before God's throne. And the books were opened, including the Book of Life. And the dead were judged according to what they had done, as recorded in the books. The sea gave up its dead, and death and the grave gave up their dead. And all were judged according to their deeds. Then death and the grave were thrown into the lake of fire. This lake of fire is the second death. And anyone whose name was not found recorded in the Book of Life was thrown into the lake of fire. (NLT)

4. Our Future Blessings:

Revelation 21:1-4 Then I saw a new heaven and a new earth, for the old heaven and the old earth had disappeared. And the sea was also gone. And I saw the holy city, the new Jerusalem, coming down from God out of heaven like a bride beautifully dressed for her husband. I heard a loud shout from the throne, saying, "Look, God's home is now among his people! He will live with them, and they will be his people. God himself will be with them. He will wipe every tear from their eyes, and there will be no more death or sorrow or crying or pain. All these things are gone forever." (NLT)

LET'S APPLY IT!

1. Be ready! Jesus is coming soon!

   Revelation 22:12 "...behold, I am coming quickly, and My reward is with Me, to give to every one according to his work."

2. Pick a side! Which side are you on?

   Revelation 20:15 ...anyone whose name was not found recorded in the Book of Life was thrown into the lake of fire. (NLT)

   Romans 10:13 "Everyone who calls on the name of the Lord will be saved!" (NIV)

3. Invite the lost to come to Christ before He returns!

    Revelation 22:17 The Spirit and the bride [church] say, "Come." Let anyone who hears this say, "Come." Let anyone who is thirsty come. Let anyone who desires drink freely from the water of life. (NLT)

ERIC DYKSTRA is the founding pastor of Free Grace United, a family of churches with locations worldwide. He also founded Free Grace Bible College, which has grown to train pastors and church leaders in several countries.

He and his wife Kelly have been married 30 years and have three children with three awesome spouses and three amazing grandchildren. If he's not teaching or hanging with his family, you can find him on a lake catching a big bass.

His other books include:

Grace on Tap: What if you didn't have to behave to make God happy with you? What if you could live the good life without a list of rules? What if God's favor was readily available to you? It's paid for, and you can have as much as you want. IT'S GRACE... ON TAP.

Unhooked & Untangled: A Guide to Finding Freedom from your Vices, Addictions, and Bad Habits

God's Perspective: 60 Important Topics and what God's Word says about them

See Christ this Christmas: A 25-day Devotional Journey

All available on Amazon.

FREE GRACE UNITED (freegrace.tv) is one church with many interdependent, grace-based congregations around the world. FGU is widely known for its unique approach to reaching those who feel the need for God's grace the most. The grace message and its accompanying Holy Spirit power are continually transforming people through this ministry.

FREE GRACE BIBLE COLLEGE (freegracebiblecollege.com) equips members of the Body of Christ to live out their calling.

www.ingramcontent.com/pod-product-compliance
Lightning Source LLC
Chambersburg PA
CBHW071217090426
42736CB00014B/2860